When Reason Sleeps

When Reason Sleeps

by
Audrey Mellard

George Ronald, Publisher
Oxford

George Ronald, *Publisher*
Oxford
www.grbooks.com

*A catalogue record for this book is available
from the British Library*

ISBN 978-0-85398-641-6

Cover design René Steiner, Steinergraphics.com

Contents

In memory of Jacob Opaade

A Note from the Author

This is Mrs Farzaneh-Moayyad's authorized version of events. All dates, details and facts have been checked. Any accounts relating to the death of Mr Farzaneh-Moayyad that have been published previously were made without reference to Mrs Farzaneh-Moayyad or any family member and may not be accurate.

Audrey Mellard

Foreword

My sincere thanks to Mrs Farzaneh-Moayyad, an incredibly brave lady who wants this story of her husband to be told. Without her patience, as we struggled to understand each other through many long sessions, it would not have been possible. I hope she will forgive any minor errors which might have slipped through.

The opening prologue is the only 'flight of fancy' I have allowed myself. We do not know for certain that 'Abdu'lláh himself witnessed the attack on the farm but someone of the family did. It is just the sort of thing that a 14-year-old might do, given that he had a gun and it was his dearest possession. I could not resist the chance to use the interesting time lapse of 100 years in this context. 'Abdu'lláh certainly told Mehrangiz about the attack as if he had seen it himself.

Some events, particularly the prison scenes, are not necessarily given here in the sequence in which they occurred, but rather as they were related to me as Mrs Moayyad remembered each incident.

Some minor encounters, i.e. with the employee from the bank and the woman on the bus, are not in strict chronological order, but upon reflection I decided to leave them as first related to me, both for simplification and for dramatic effect.

Some locations have been deliberately left vague, as in the escape route used, since to give too many details might endanger anyone involved in similar efforts.

Similarly, most names have not been given, especially for the young trainee medic who escaped at the same time and whose relatives might still be in Iran.

Acknowledgements

Grateful thanks to Mrs Farzaneh-Moayyad's eldest son, Farshid, for the time he spent translating her original notes from Farsi into English and in conversations with his mother. Thanks also are due to Farshid's wife, Rose, for her uncomplaining support when so much of his precious leisure time was spent on this project.

Many thanks to Roshanak for her thoughtful and careful response to my questions. Thanks also to Fardin for giving up so much of his time to help clarify details. Thanks are also due to the late Dr Arthur Lister for his professional advice on medical matters. Thanks to Farhad and Carrie Varjavandi for information about Farhad's parents, and to Moojan and Wendi Momen.

Finally, a very special 'thank you' to my husband Keith, without whose constant encouragement and technical expertise this effort might have come to nothing.

Audrey Mellard

Part One

'The sleep of reason . . .'

1

Persia 1884 to Geneva 1988

It was that hour before the dawn when there is no colour in the landscape . . . that mysterious time between darkness and sunrise, when the only light in the sky is a pearly, misty grey, and the whole world seems to sleep. 'Abdu'lláh stayed crouched behind the old stone wall until long after the mob had left. Now the fires were dying out, and in the moonlight the smoking ruins of the house were clearly to be seen. All the animals were dead. The cattle had been driven into the old cowshed and the stout door securely fastened. The tubs of butter from the dairy had been poured over them and lighted torches thrown in to ignite it. The memory of the anguished bellowing of the trapped animals, and the stench of burning hair and flesh, would stay with 'Abdu'lláh for the rest of his life.

He was 14 years old and that day had disobeyed his father for the first time in his life. When the mayor of the nearby village had sent warning early in the morning that the local mullá had been inciting the villagers to 'rise up and destroy the infidels in our midst', his father had realized that he must get his wife and young children to safety as quickly as possible. There was no time to pack anything, and almost everything that they owned had to be left behind.

'Abdu'lláh's disobedience happened when he remembered that his most precious possession, his gun, was missing. It had been his birthday present earlier that year, and he spent a great deal of time lavishing care on it, polishing the beautifully chased stock, and cleaning the barrel carefully. He was already a good shot and the rifle meant a great deal to him. When he realized it had been left behind, he had simply slipped away from the family and returned to the house.

He had had only enough time to retrieve the gun and get out of the house when he heard the mob approaching. He concealed himself behind a wall, rubbing dirt onto his clothes and the stock of the gun so that no glint of moonlight would reflect in it and betray his hiding place. He prayed that his father and mother and the younger children had got safely away. He also prayed that his father would not return to try to find him. He wept when he realized that his disobedience might have endangered them all.

'Abdu'lláh could not understand why the people he had known all his life now seemed to hate them so much. He had believed them to be his friends. He played with their children. His father and his mother had helped almost all of them at one time or another, when anyone was sick, or needed advice with their problems, or in hard times when there was very little food to be had. They had always come to consult with his father, knowing that his wise counsel would help them to find a way to deal with whatever was troubling them. Now they were so hated that the villagers would even destroy the beasts and the dairy produce rather than take them for themselves.

It would perhaps have been understandable if 'Abdu'lláh had decided to use his gun to shoot them all, but this was not an option for him. The new religion of his father – the cause of the mullá's hatred – strictly forbad the taking of another human life. Indeed, his father had told him it was better that a man should die rather than kill another, for all men were brothers and should strive to live in peace and unity with each other. The time was coming when 'the Kingdom of God on earth' would be established in the world, and peace and harmony would be the normal state of affairs for all mankind.

All these ideas were new and strange but 'Abdu'lláh could not wait to be 15 when he would be old enough to choose for himself to become a member of this new Faith. It was no longer enough, his father had explained, merely to follow the religion of one's parents; it was up to the individual to decide for himself the right path to follow. This new religion of his father and grandfather also taught that there was no longer any need for clergy to interpret the word of God for the people. It was the responsibility of each and every individual to find out what was required of them by reading the words of God for themselves and living their lives according to the laws given to them in this new Dispensation. Maybe this independence of thought was another reason why the people had turned against them?

Eventually 'Abdu'lláh realized that the men had left.

The fires were almost out and the smoke had drifted away. There was still a horrible smell from the burnt cattle in the shed, where the roof had gone and the door still smouldered, but there was no sound from inside and he knew they were all dead.

Cautiously he flexed his cramped limbs and crept warily out of his hiding place, poised to flee at any sound. No one was there. In that bleak dawn, as he surveyed the ruination of everything his father and his grandfathers had worked for all their lives, the 14 year old 'Abdu'lláh would never have imagined that the next hundred years would see his descendants scattered across the globe. They would live in Australia and England, in the USA and Canada, in France and Scotland. He could never have dreamt that his youngest daughter, who would not be born until he was 65, would one day fly in a yet to be invented jet to Switzerland to give a report on the execution of her husband, who died simply because he was a member of the Bahá'í Faith, to a human rights committee of a yet to be formed international organization dedicated to the promotion of universal peace and co-operation.

This is her story . . . and his . . .

London, England, 1988

Mehri boarded the plane alone. There was no one to see her off but she knew that in Geneva there would be someone to meet her, and the thought gave her confidence. To her relief, nobody showed any interest in her as she found her seat and settled down. It was the first time in her life she had flown alone but not the first time she had flown, so she knew exactly what to expect as the cabin crew went through the safety drill, and the instruction to 'fasten seatbelts' flashed up before take-off. In the early years of her marriage she had travelled with her husband, and later with their children, on several trips abroad, visiting the European capitals of London, Paris and Rome. They had also been to Turkey, Yugoslavia and Czechoslovakia, amongst other places, so she was certainly no stranger to air travel.

On this occasion she carefully avoided eye contact with fellow passengers. She was still too afraid to want any contact with strangers; even a friendly smile was almost beyond her. The strains of the last few years had left her wary even of the kindness of strangers, for she feared people like that mysterious woman who once had forced her into conversation on a bus, but had only wanted to assuage her own conscience, regardless of the nightmares her 'confession' would leave behind.

The effort of finding her way about the airport – coping with the check-in system, boarding the plane, finding a seat, stowing away the small case which was the only luggage she was taking with her – had left her feeling exhausted and unwell. When a stewardess appeared and spoke to her, she shrank back in the seat. She knew that she ought to understand what the woman was saying but the words did not make any sense. She had studied English at school and had been living in the UK for at least two years now, but it was as if she had never heard a word spoken before. Patiently, the stewardess repeated her query, in French this time, and she recognized the language, but never having studied it, was unable to reply. She wished she had her husband with her. He had been for many years in the employment of a French company and spoke the language beautifully. The stewardess tried, again, in English, and this time she understood.

'Thank you,' she replied, in the same language. 'I will have some water, please.' Even the fleeting thought of her husband had been a mistake, she found, as she suddenly had to struggle to maintain her composure, but she sipped the water and hoped her momentary lapse had gone unnoticed. She knew that soon she would have to face relating all the details of her husband's story, the truth about his life and death, all the tiny relevant details that made up the whole, however distressing it would be for her, for that was the sole purpose of this journey to Geneva.

The thought of the coming interrogation suddenly filled her with dread. She knew that was illogical, for 'interrogation' was hardly the right word for what was going to happen. This time, she had been invited to tell her story to a United Nations Committee on Human Rights. This time, she would be treated with respect. It would not be remotely like being in prison. This time there would be boxes of tissues available if she wept, and cups of tea, to cater for her needs. People supporting her with love and concern. She would try not to think of her husband just yet, she decided, resolutely turning her thoughts to her children.

She was happy that all three were safe and well. Only time would tell if they had suffered any lasting psychological damage from the terrible events that had engulfed their family, and about that she was powerless to do anything except to love them all, pray for them and try to keep them focused on the positive aspects of life. People thought that because the two boys, young men now, had been sent abroad to study, they had been safely out of the way and therefore relatively untouched by the experiences of their parents and little sister. This was not so, she knew, and the thought of their lost youth made her want to weep. They had been forced to become adults and independent long before they were ready for it, and both had suffered accordingly, mainly in silence, with only each other to turn to for comfort. The helplessness of those in such situations is almost impossible to comprehend.

She thought of her daughter, Roshanak, known to family and friends as 'Shanna'. Beautiful and spirited, she had shown great courage and resilience throughout all their tribulations, but she had not survived entirely unscathed. Shanna had been refused admission to one school after another. When in school she had often been bullied, usually by teachers, but had refused to be cowed, standing up to them bravely and declaring fiercely that she was proud of her father. When her mother was in prison she had been passed from the care of one relative to another, or to friends, all of whom had their own problems and, while deeply concerned for her welfare, could give little practical help to a traumatized child whose beloved father had been murdered, whose very sick mother was in prison under sentence of death, who for months had not been allowed even to visit her mother, and whose much-loved aunt had earlier been arrested and simply 'disappeared', never to be seen or heard of again.

As the plane flew steadily on its way, Mehrangiz Farzaneh-Moayyad – Mehri to her friends – sat lost in her own thoughts. She had not been able to relax enough to make any contact with other passengers, one or two of whom had tried to chat with her. Perhaps some of them were intrigued by their quiet fellow passenger and wondered idly why she was travelling alone. Her pale, clear skin and fine bone structure, her obvious extreme exhaustion, seemed to indicate that here was someone recently, but not quite, recovered from some debilitating illness. Was she really fit to travel?

As the plane circled Geneva on its approach to landing, there was a glimpse of the expanse of blue lake with the Alps beyond, then the red roofs of the town, and all the beautiful green spaces of the parks and gardens came into view, ordered and peaceful, and shining in the sun. To Mehri it looked like another world, one so far removed from the world she had escaped from that it was almost hard to believe it was part of the same planet.

As she gathered her few belongings together, one of the stewardesses who had looked after her with great kindness asked if she was to be met. Would she be all right? Grateful for the concern, Mehri thanked her and assured her that she did indeed expect to be met.

She had come to Geneva to fulfil an obligation placed upon her, and she intended to do her very best for the people who no longer had a voice in this world to speak for themselves. She did not say any of this to the stewardess of course, but braced herself mentally for the task ahead and prepared to disembark. Mehri left the plane as she had boarded it, unnoticed by the majority of her fellow travellers. An unremarkable woman in herself, perhaps, but one with a most remarkable story to tell, a story both of horror and hope.

2

Mehrangiz

Mehrangiz Samadani was born in Iran in 1935, when her father, 'Abdu'lláh, was 65 years old, and already a grandfather. Within two years of the attack on the family property, which he had witnessed as a boy of 14, both his parents were dead and he had assumed responsibility for the four younger children. His older sister was already married and living in Turkey with her husband. The family had been reduced to very straitened circumstances in the immediate aftermath of the attack; to such a degree that one day, about six months after his father had died from a sudden heart attack, 'Abdu'lláh returned home to find that his mother had sold his precious gun to buy food for them all. She was extremely upset at having done this, but she had succumbed to the persuasiveness of one of the itinerant 'merchants' who prey on the poor, travelling from town to town and knocking on doors to ask if the householder has anything of value to sell. They are eager to purchase gold, jewellery or any precious objects, but always at scandalously low prices, little short of robbery. The gun had cost a great deal of money. 'Abdu'lláh's poor mother had received only about a fiftieth of its cost. She was extremely distressed at having sold the gun for only a fraction of its value, but she had been desperate to buy food for the children. It is more than likely that the stress of their circumstances and the deprivation that brought them to near starvation contributed to the early deaths of both parents. When his mother died, little more than a year after her husband, 'Abdu'lláh became responsible for all the younger children. He had already been found employment as a jeweller to help to provide for them all. At this time the daughter of neighbours was sent to the house to help him look after the children, but as it was thought unseemly for two unrelated young people to be living under the same roof, they were obliged to marry, whether they really wanted to or not. This was not so unusual in a society where arranged marriages were the norm. He was 16 and his wife a little older. Fortunately, it seems to have been a happy union and they eventually had several children together. After her death, 'Abdu'lláh married again. Mehrangiz was his youngest child with his second wife.

When Mehri was born the family was living in Qazvin, a market town less than a hundred miles northwest of the capital, Tehran. The Iran into which Mehri was born was a society that was just entering a period of social and economic modernization. For nearly 80 years, the savage persecution of the Bábís, the followers of the Báb, and the Bahá'ís, who had followed Bahá'u'lláh after His disclosure of His station in 1863, had raged almost unchecked.

Reza Khan Pahlavi had led a successful coup against the ruling Qajar dynasty in 1921 and had been crowned Shah in 1925. It was his intention to modernize his country and many sweeping reforms, centred on Tehran, were introduced. Electricity replaced oil and gas for lighting.

Streets were widened and surfaced. Beautiful squares were laid out, with fountains and flowerbeds and statues. But this was often at the expense of old families, particularly those of the previous dynasty, whose ancestral homes were demolished to make room for the Shah's schemes.

At that time much of the country had no modern road network and most areas were reached only by roads that were little more than dirt tracks, which were often washed away in heavy rainstorms. Indeed, as late as the 1970s, one of 'Abdu'lláh's great grandsons died when his car, a heavy Mercedes-Benz, was washed into a ravine in just such conditions.

In Europe surnames had been in common use since at least as early as the 13th century but in Iran it was not until 1925 that Reza Shah required all citizens to adopt surnames and obtain birth certificates for their children. Prior to this, most people had only a first name and some indication of who they were or where they came from. When the order to adopt surnames was given, many people wanted to use their place of birth or residence as their new surname. So many wanted to choose the same name, that the official in charge of issuing the surnames would arbitrarily decide that one particular name had been used enough. That was how it happened that brothers could be given different names, especially if they did not attend at the same time. Some people had no idea what name to take and were happy to leave it to the officials, who were often quite frivolous in the names they allocated. Hitherto, girls had been known only as daughter, or sister, or wife of someone whose name followed theirs. Now at least they would have a family name. Similarly, birth dates were very hit-or-miss, usually related to the seasons, or some memorable event such as an earthquake or a violent storm.

In 1935, the year of Mehri's birth, the veil was banned. It was forbidden for women to cover themselves in the chador, a large, concealing piece of cloth which covered the shoulders, forehead and chin and revealed only eyes, nose and mouth. The full veil, where only the eyes can be seen, had never been in common use in Persia. Reza Shah's reforms were very sudden and the edict was the cause of real distress to some of the women who had never known anything else. They felt shockingly exposed, and some refused to leave their homes for many weeks. At least one husband got round the problem by ordering the largest-brimmed Parisian hats he could find for all the ladies of his household, and insisting they drive out with him, to accustom them to the public gaze.

In 1935, too, the name of the country formally changed. Persia is the name that has come down through history in the West, an illustrious name redolent with stories of ancient heroes and battles, for Persia had an empire a thousand years before the foundation of the city of Rome, and once enjoyed great renown. Records show that as early as 500 BC Persian gardens in the courtyards of some of the houses were fragrant with roses, shaded with trees and green plants, and cooled by running water. By the late 19th century those early glories, except for beautiful roses and gardens, had completely disappeared, the empire was long gone, and Persia had deteriorated, the mass of the people uneducated, with no access to education, and the rights of women completely denied. At the same time, a very few families had amassed for themselves vast wealth, almost beyond imagining, and this they would not be ready to relinquish willingly.

The Shah in 1935 asked that those countries having diplomatic relations with his country use the name which its people had always called it, Iran, rather than Persia, the name by which it was formally known in the West. The people were to be called Iranians, to include all the different ethnic groups existing in Iran, rather than the name of it largest group, Persians. To this day, many people have not become accustomed to being 'Iranian', and prefer to be known as 'Persian'.

The reforms of the new Shah removed much power from the clerics, his intention being to turn the constitution into a secular one. A judiciary was created, under a Ministry of Justice, with courts, judges and lawyers. Until then, justice, like education, had been in the hands of the clergy and the religious courts. Naturally the change caused great upset and opposition from the religious leaders, even though the new Civil Code was not intended to oppose Sharia, the Islamic law. From this time, violent opposition to the Bahá'ís occurred only sporadically, and mainly in the rural areas. It may have been helpful that in 1925 a court case in Egypt, a Muslim country, had recognized the Bahá'í Faith as an independent world religion and not a sect of Islam. However, prejudice against the Bahá'ís remained an unpleasant fact of life, manifested in various ways. Mehri remembers that one night when she was very young, they returned late from a Bahá'í meeting, and her mother was unable to open the door because the handle had been smeared in dog mess. Not the most pleasant 'welcome home' for anyone to experience, and Mehri has never forgotten her poor mother's disgust and distress.

It was unfortunate that in December 1934 the reforming zeal of the Shah, who was determined to take Iran into the 20th century by removing the influence of religion, caused the closure of the two Tarbíyat schools in Tehran, one for boys and one for girls, that were very popular with all classes of people. In 1934 the Ministry of Education demanded that the schools remain open on the nine Bahá'í holy days, using the pretext that the Bahá'í Faith was not officially recognized. When the schools closed on the next holy day, the government refused permission for the schools to re-open afterwards.

The Bahá'í emphasis on education, particularly for girls, who in time will become mothers and the first educators of their children, made the Bahá'ís very eager to run their own schools, which were open to everyone.

In this period the Bahá'ís also established clinics and hospitals and their children were free to go to university. There were very few restrictions on jobs they could do and many became civil servants. Because of the moral code they chose to live by, the Bahá'ís became known for their honesty and uprightness and were generally regarded as model employees. Following the Bahá'í laws, they chose to have no involvement in politics. In accordance with the laws of Bahá'u'lláh, they chose to be monogamous, at a time when this was not the norm in the country. Eventually the Shah proclaimed polygamy illegal and declared that henceforth women were to be equal and that a man could have only one wife.

From the time she was born, Mehri enjoyed a normal, happy childhood. Home was a 300-year-old family house where most of her many older siblings had been born. At least one of her siblings, a doctor, had died before she was born. Life was comfortable enough at that time. The small family farm produced crops of grapes and tea and pistachio nuts and almost everything else that they needed. She remembers that her mother prepared all their food herself, preserving for winter use the abundant crops of pomegranates and grapes grown on the farm. Mehri says that they bought almost nothing from shops except bread and milk and meat. Everything else that was needed they made or grew themselves. She remembers watching her mother at all sorts of household tasks but whenever she tried to help she would be told to get on with her studies! Grapes in particular were used and preserved in a variety of ways. Huge bundles would be tied with ropes and hung in the attic roof until needed. This ensured a plentiful supply of sultanas and raisins throughout the year. Alcohol was never made because it is forbidden in the Bahá'í Faith, as it is in Islam, but there was always plenty of freshly pressed grape juice available. Her mother also made a delicious soft purée with grapes. It was sweet like honey and if mixed with snow was almost like ice cream. She also made vinegar from red grapes, and a sharp pickle, to add piquancy to their meat dishes.

Mehri also remembers the comfort of snuggling under thick blankets and quilts as they gathered for warmth round the korsi, a sort of low table under which a charcoal brazier burnt slowly, the embers covered with a thick layer of ashes which ensured an even distribution of heat and prevented burning. They sat on cushions around it with hands and feet tucked under the blankets. When it was really cold they slept beside it at night and at mealtimes the top could be used as a table. This sounds like a terrible fire risk but accident statistics for this particular household installation were never recorded and Mehri denies all knowledge of any problems ever caused by this system.

The house was heated by wood burning stoves, the smoke going through a series of pipes in the walls and out through the roof.

Mehri's father was keenly interested in the welfare of all his children. He wanted his daughters to be as well-educated as his sons and for them all to be able to make their way in the world. When the opportunity was available, he urged them to go on to university. He always encouraged them to develop any talents they might have, and sometimes these were quite novel. For instance, Mehri was urged to develop her singing voice by practising in an enormous brick and clay underground water cistern which served as a resonance chamber. This produced different sounds at different times, presumably depending on the level of water in it. Mehri also remembers lessons from him on deportment, explaining how, in accordance with the custom of the time, a young lady should conduct herself, both in public and in private, for instance, by not laughing out loud in public.

Mehri enjoyed her schooldays very much, but there was a lot of name-calling amongst the children, particularly when they were all very young. As religious minorities, the Jews and Christians were targets as often as the Bahá'ís, but when they were small most of them simply called names back. One boy in Mehri's class was a regular tormentor of all of them. Many years later, when visiting her daughter in Australia, Mehri met this boy again. He was delighted to see her and laughed as he apologized for his youthful transgressions. They were at a Bahá'í meeting and he was pleased to be able to tell her he was now married to a Bahá'í!

Once, in school, Mehri was made to read out a chapter of a history book entitled 'The Báb's Plot'. She politely changed the title to 'The Báb's Declaration' and explained to the teacher that she was correcting the text because it was all wrong. The teacher was not very pleased with her and complained to her parents.

When children were about the age of 12, schooling became single-sex and Mehri was sent to an all-girls lycée for the next five or six years. Persian language and literature are both heavily influenced by Arabic and at the lycée the study of that language was compulsory for all pupils. They had a choice of English or French for another foreign language and Mehri opted for English. The curriculum placed great emphasis on the physical aspects of their education and Mehri talks enthusiastically of playing netball and volleyball, and of taking part in gymnastics. She also played table tennis. Once, she was part of a school team that prepared a dancing display for distinguished visitors. Dressed in sailor suits, the girls danced a hornpipe for the Shah and his party. This was quite a memorable occasion for all the children involved.

As the schools were organized on the French system, on completion of their studies the pupils were awarded a Baccalaureate. Mehri left with her high school diploma in science and prepared to continue her studies at university.

3

Marriage

When Mehri was 18, 'Abdu'lláh died. It was 1953 and he was 83 years old.

The situation in Iran had seemed reasonably stable for several years although the Bahá'ís had suffered persecution across the country in this period. In 1941 Reza Shah had abdicated in favour of his son, Mohammad Reza Pahlavi. The new Shah tried to institute many social reforms and move away from the old concept of the monarchy, but this upset many of his countrymen. In 1951 the new prime minister, Mohammad Mosaddegh, nationalized the Anglo-Iranian Oil Company, creating international difficulties for the government. Eventually, Mosaddegh was ousted by a coup in 1953, imprisoned for three years and released to house arrest in 1956.

It was during this period of unrest that the persecution of the Bahá'ís escalated, with prominent religious leaders calling for the suppression of the religion and for the destruction of their property. In 1955, an anti-Bahá'í campaign was launched, with a cleric who was a skilled orator giving fiery speeches daily on the radio during the month of fasting. This incited a wave of violence against Bahá'ís across the country, including the destruction of the Bahá'í National Centre in Tehran. High-ranking army officers and clerics were photographed taking turns with a pickaxe to destroy the Centre's dome. The Minister of the Interior announced in the Parliament that the government had issued orders for the suppression of the Bahá'í Faith, unleashing a new wave of violence and bloodshed. In the same year the House of the Báb in Shiraz, the home where He had first announced His station to a seeker in 1844 and later a place of pilgrimage for Bahá'ís from around the world, was attacked and desecrated for a second time. It was later carefully and lovingly restored. Reports of the attacks against the Bahá'ís were carried by newspapers in many countries.

The nation-wide persecution of the Bahá'í community continued unchecked without official investigation and the members of the religion had no protection under the law as it stood. The Bahá'í International Community then launched a campaign to highlight what was happening to the Bahá'ís. The Bahá'í International Community delegates presented their case to the United Nations and the Secretary-General intervened. United Nations Secretary-General Dag Hammarskjold met with the Iranian Minister of Foreign Affairs and brought an immediate end to the physical persecution and lifted the danger of a massacre. Subsequently, some of the confiscated Bahá'í properties were returned to their rightful owners.

Except for the loss of her father, and the sadness she shared with her fellow Bahá'ís, none of this impinged directly on Mehri. She intended to continue her studies and life went on almost as normal. Not long after her father's death, she was introduced to the man who would soon become her husband.

Manuchihr Farzaneh-Moayyad was from a very similar background to her own, coming from a Bahá'í family whose history went back to the very beginning of the Bahá'í Faith. The stepmother who brought him up from babyhood was herself descended from one of the very first followers of the Báb, known as the 'Letters of the Living', the first 18 people to recognize the divine station of the Báb of their own accord. Like the 12 disciples who had first recognized Jesus Christ and followed Him against all opposition, these 17 men and one woman had been given the responsibility of spreading the message of the new revelation as far and as widely as possible.

Mehri tells an interesting story from this time, passed down to her from her husband's family:

> Some of the Báb's disciples were discussing the magnitude of their task, given the state of Persia in 1844. They asked the Báb, 'Your Holiness, we can go on foot, or we can ride on a donkey, but how are we to cover the distances involved? It will take several lifetimes for us to get this message round the world!'
>
> The Báb is said to have replied along these lines (paraphrased), 'Do not worry. Energy has now been released into the world that will provide a worldwide system of communications.'

We not do know if the story is true but the date of the declaration of the Báb was the evening of 22 May 1844. On 24 May that same year, Samuel Morse, in America, sent the first telegraph message in his new code. And the message? 'What hath God wrought?'

From that beginning, the speed of the development of all forms of communications has been truly astonishing and making the world evermore interconnected. We have seen our beautiful blue planet from outer space, an awe-inspiring sight that no earlier generations have had the privilege of seeing. We have watched as men walked on the moon, and wept as other astronauts died in the attempt to reach it. All this has happened in a very short space of human development.

As to the marriage, the story as Mehri tells it was that Manuchihr was visiting a cousin of hers one day and saw Mehri's photograph. He was immediately smitten, declaring that this was the girl he wanted to marry and spend the rest of his life with. The cousin tried to tease him, saying that the photograph was of a very old aunt when she was younger, or something of the sort. Manuchihr would have none of it and eventually the cousin relented and introduced them, reminding him that as Mehri was still in mourning, she was unlikely to be interested in the young man. However, the attraction was mutual. Mehri was 19 when they married in a simple Bahá'í ceremony, and Manuchihr nearly eight years older.

4

Family

Before their eldest son, Farshid, was born in 1958, Mehri and Manuchihr suffered the distress of three miscarriages in a relatively short time. This forced Mehri to seek a consultation with a specialist gynaecologist, a Dr Mosaddegh, who she believes was the son of the former prime minister. He was an ardent socialist, possibly even communist in his political views, and used to tease Mehri about the delicate state of her hands, which he said were obviously not accustomed to manual labour or to holding a gun! Whatever his politics, he was first of all a good doctor and eventually they rejoiced in the safe arrival of their first child. Their second son, Fardin, was born in 1962 and in 1970 the family was completed with the arrival of a daughter, Roshanak, or Shanna, as she usually preferred to be called.

Life for the young family was happy and comfortable at that time. Wherever they lived, their home was always open to all their friends and relatives, for they enjoyed entertaining. The children did well at school and it was clear from an early age that they would all be capable of going to university. This was very pleasing to their parents who, like most parents everywhere, wanted them to realize their full potential. However, there were often unpleasant reminders that as members of a minority religion in Iran, albeit the largest minority, nothing could be taken for granted – there was always an undercurrent.

When Farshid was very young, perhaps about a year old, they had a narrow escape one day when driving in the mountains. Bandits attacked them and tried to force Manuchihr to stop the car. He yelled at Mehri to keep her head down and kept going. The bullets shattered the windscreen and just missed Manuchihr but he drove faster and got them all safely away. In retrospect it sounds very exciting but it must have been extremely alarming at the time.

Farshid was still quite young, probably about 18 months old, when he was taken to visit his paternal grandfather in Tehran. The house there was heated by oil-filled stoves, very plain, basic metal things. Farshid was warned not to touch because they were extremely hot. Presumably to test the validity of this, he very carefully took his grandfather's finger and touched it to the stove. Grandfather jumped and said, 'Ouch!' Farshid was delighted with this reaction. His grandfather tried not to laugh, not wishing to relinquish his image of the stern patriarch. Farshid was about four when this grandfather died, before his brother and sister were born.

When Farshid started school, it was not long before his parents were summoned to see his teacher, who complained that he had called other children 'dirty Muslim dogs'. A dog is regarded as the dirtiest of animals in Islam, so this is a very insulting thing to say.

When asked to explain this, Farshid replied, 'They (the other children) called me "dirty Bahá'í dog" so I called them the same bad name.'

The teacher seemed to think that the offence was all his. This reminded Mehri of when she had first started school, and her mother had gone to see her teacher to complain that her little daughter was being called 'a dirty Bahá'í dog' by some of her classmates, and to ask for this to be stopped. On that occasion the teacher had shrugged her shoulders and said, 'The children are right. How can I tell them not to?' So nothing had changed in that respect.

Roshanak demonstrated a lively, enquiring, independent mind from a very early age. When she was about four years old she asked her mother, 'Well, where is God? You are always telling me about Him, can we see Him? Can you show Him to me, please?'

Mehri racked her brains for a simple way to explain the universality of the concept of God to her little daughter. Meanwhile, Shanna pursued her own lines of enquiry. She went to her father with the same questions. She asked each of her brothers, in turn.

'Have you seen God? Where is He?'

She asked her aunts and uncles and cousins. She asked anyone and everyone she met. No one could satisfy her until Mehri had an idea. Taking her outside on a very windy day she showed her the trees and the flowers moving in the breeze. She pointed out to Shanna that she could feel the wind in her hair and blowing her skirts about, and could see that across the street it was making little eddies in the dust.

'Can you see the wind?' she asked her. 'Can you catch the wind? Can you touch the wind?' To all these questions Shanna replied, 'No.'

Mehri explained that the wind is undoubtedly there, even though she could not see it, or feel it or touch it. It was obviously touching Shanna, the proof was in her blowing hair and skirt, and she could see it in the moving trees. Mehri then explained that the presence of God is like the wind, those who believe know it is there, without the physical proof of being able to see or touch or hold anything.

Shanna had a difficult time at school. She started school at six, when she was told that if she did not follow the custom and cover her hair she would go to hell. This was both frightening and threatening. In order to register for school a form had to be completed and the question-naire always included the child's religion. To put 'Bahá'í' meant that a child might not be accepted by the school. Any child of a Bahá'í, no matter what age, was considered a Bahá'í by the authorities, even though that child may have chosen not to be one at the age of 15, the age of spiritual maturity when a person decides for herself what her religion is. Even if someone tried to amend the forms to get her accepted, Shanna would proudly alter them to declare herself a 'Bahá'í'.

When she was 11, a Jewish school was found for Shanna. Here she told the other children that she was a Bahá'í, and that in her religion they were allowed – no, expected – to learn about other religions and then choose for themselves which they wanted to follow. The religious education teacher spoke about Islam.

One of the children asked, 'Can we read about other religions?'

The teacher (in the Jewish school) replied, 'Oh, yes! Islam is very pure and respects other religions!'

The child asked, 'And what if we decide we don't want to be Muslim?'

'Then you would be an atheist and deserve to be killed!'

Shanna asked, 'What is the point of reading then?'

For this comment she was beaten about the head. She was often hit by the teachers for defending her religion.

On another occasion, the religious education teacher spoke of Muhammad's sufferings. Shanna then shared the Bahá'í concept that all Manifestations have suffered to bring God's message to the people and no power on earth can stop the Cause of God. For this she was again beaten about the head and told to 'shut up'. A few days later the same teacher told her not to mention the Bahá'í Faith again. Shanna replied that she was not afraid or ashamed to be Bahá'í, and she never would be.

All the three children reported similar instances of prejudice throughout their schooldays but they all insisted that their parents request that they be given time off school for the holy days. Even if the requests were not granted, at least the schools knew that Bahá'ís have their own holy days. Whatever problems there might be outside the home, they were always happy and secure at home.

Manuchihr was always very generous to others. In the early days of their marriage he sponsored two families who were trying to spread the Bahá'í teachings but lacked resources. He would take home his salary and carefully divide it into three. When Farshid was born, Mehri asked him, 'Can't our share be a little bigger?'

He replied, 'No, we have only one child, they each have three.'

On another occasion when he was sending money to someone in need, at a time when they had not much for themselves, he said, 'That little won't make me a prince or a pauper but it might make a big difference to him.'

Manuchihr had a natural aptitude for fixing all things mechanical, from the car to the plumbing, but was slightly less adept when it came to the natural world. When the two eldest children were young, and safely out of the way with Mehri one day, he decided to remove a wasp's nest that he had spotted on the side of the house, because he was sure it was a danger to the children. He thought he would get it done while he was alone. First, he poked it with a stick. Whether this was to gauge the strength of the wasps' objections he never explained but they definitely did not like it. When Mehri returned home there was an unrecognizable stranger in their bedroom, with her doctor brother in attendance. Manuchihr had been stung so badly that his face was completely distorted and he was very ill. He had only just managed to call his brother-in-law for assistance before collapsing. What a fright he gave them all. Later they had to seek outside help to remove the nest. Manuchihr was usually much more careful, and much luckier, than that.

Another lucky escape came when he was the manager of a French–Iranian dam building project, which his brother had asked Manuchihr to run for him. Explosives were set to go off and everything was supposed to be in order but he was not confident that his car was quite out of range. He left his office to move the car and the office he had just vacated was crushed by falling rocks dropping onto the roof – which was not in accordance with anyone's calculations!

On another occasion he was driving on the road to Tehran when he suddenly stopped, thinking there was something wrong with the car. He found nothing but a stone in the wheel, which was not a problem. Only a short distance ahead, however, he found that a landslide had come down on the road, right where his car would probably have been had not some instinct made him stop to look at the wheel.

On yet another occasion, the Shah was to make an official visit to Shiraz. For reason he could not explain, Manuchihr was extremely reluctant to attend this welcome party and managed to find a good reason to be 'out of town' on the day. This was eventually to prove very fortunate indeed, because after the overthrow of the Shah in 1979, everyone who had attended this reception was rounded up and executed by the Revolutionary Government, attendance being taken as 'proof' of their support for the Shah and his regime.

There was another sort of official occasion, a reception, again in 1979, to which Manuchihr and Mehri were invited. The highlight was to be a tour of a new aircraft carrier recently purchased for the navy. This invitation was not from the Shah but from a cousin of Mehri. Roshanak and Fardin went with them. Mehri was presented with a bouquet of roses, which Shanna was pleased to carry for her. The ship was vast, with long corridors disappearing into the distance, where it was easy for an imaginative child to fear they might get lost. Her parents had no need to worry, for the resourceful Shanna thoughtfully dropped rose petals all along their path, to provide a trail for them to follow, if need be.

Shanna remembers thinking, as she was dropping the petals, 'Mum will not like me doing this!' But instead of telling her off for making a mess, they were all very happy to use her trail to find the way out.

5

Manuchihr

Looking at the very few family photographs that have survived, reading his documents and talking to his family, it is possible to build a picture of Manuchihr, a nice-looking young man, handsome almost, broad-shouldered and stocky, a man torn from his family in the very prime of life, who was not to be allowed to live to see his children reach adulthood, and who would be deprived of the joy of knowing his grandchildren and sharing with them his own unique experiences. The stories about his life, treasured vignettes which keep his memory alive in his family, and the many accounts of how he dealt with people and the situations he encountered, create a clear picture of a generous man, who was incapable of dishonesty or deceit, a very loyal and loving man. He was responsible, reputable, just and fair; completely trustworthy and dependable, and brave enough to put his life on the line for what he believed in, when it was asked of him

Manuchihr's grandfather had been the highest ranking Islamic cleric in Isfahan, and his father also became a Muslim cleric at one time, before he became a member of the Bahá'í Faith. Mehri remembers her father-in-law as a very serious, very severe person, not one to be 'messed about' with. No one sat in his presence unless instructed to do so. He was a strict disciplinarian with a strong sense of duty. His own father had not been noted for his sense of humour, and Manuchihr's father's own joyless upbringing had reflected this.

There is a story told in the family of the time Manuchihr's father, or it might have been his grandfather, was a young teacher in a Zoroastrian school in Tehran where he taught Arabic. Family folklore relates that one of his students was a prince, a son of Reza Shah, but it is more likely that he was a scion of the previously ruling Qajar dynasty since Reza Khan Pahlavi was crowned Shah in 1925, only two years before Manuchihr himself was born. This boy was never disciplined at home, or at school, and expected to be allowed to do as he pleased. He was not a particularly bad child, just something of a mischief who expected to get his own way all the time, as he was allowed to do at home. On this occasion, the teacher saw a reflection in his spectacles of the prince mocking him behind his back. He turned around and slapped the boy for his disrespect. The school was in an uproar.

'We will be closed down! You will be executed! We will all be executed!'

Fortunately, the boy's father was a sensible man. He sent the teacher a note and a gold coin as a reward. The note read, 'Thank you for making a real effort to educate my son! He will perhaps behave better now.'

There was very little laughter in the home where Manuchihr grew up and this was one of the reasons why he was determined to enjoy a more relaxed relationship with his own children. He wanted his children to have a more satisfying, fulfilling life than he had had as a child.

Manuchihr remembered a time when he was about ten years old. One of his sisters and Bahíyyih Nádirí, the young wife of his eldest brother, were laughing and joking with each other. The sound of their laughter enraged Manuchihr's father, who firmly believed that modest women should not laugh out loud and that it was the duty of a good father to help them develop dignity and decorum. He chased them with a stick, threatening to chastise them. They fled and locked themselves in a bathroom, out of his reach, still giggling. He then chased Manuchihr instead for making them laugh. His father was so cross that he was stammering and Manuchihr had to finish his sentences for him, which fortunately made the old man laugh, diffusing the situation. The stern, unbending figure that Manuchihr had always known was perhaps beginning to mellow with age by the time Farshid was born, so that his delighted reaction when Farshid touched his finger to the hot stove was not so amazing as it would have been a decade or so earlier.

They had been married for several years before Manuchihr remembered to tell Mehrangiz that the woman she knew as his mother was actually his step-mother and had brought him up from babyhood. Like Mehri, he was the youngest child in the family, having five brothers and sisters. His father had had a great deal of contact with the Bahá'ís in Isfahan at one time and had fallen in love with, and married, a Bahá'í girl. He became a Bahá'í himself but did not dare tell any of his family at that time. In the Bahá'í Faith, all living parents must freely give their consent to the marriage of their children, otherwise the marriage cannot take place, but this requirement was possibly not widely known in those early days. His relatives did not realize he had actually become a member of the hated Bahá'í Faith, as they saw it, until he and his wife, who was a descendant of one of the disciples of the Báb, already had five children. When his family finally learned that he had been a Bahá'í for several years, they plotted to kill him 'for bringing such shame on the family'.

The threat was very real. He was forced to flee, leaving his wife and children behind, and went to Tehran. He was there for nearly three years before he thought it safe enough to send for his wife and children to join him. When his wife arrived, she found that he had, according to Islamic custom, taken a second wife, a Muslim woman, and had a seven-month-old son, Manuchihr. Iranian Bahá'ís at that time were not fully aware of the Bahá'í teaching that they were not to take a second spouse while married to the first, and many still followed the local customs. The head of the Faith, Shoghi Effendi, gradually implemented this law. Some, in their ardour to obey the Bahá'í law, thought they had to divorce their second wives, even though Shoghi Effendi clarified that this was not the case. But communication was difficult and the messages were not always received, so many suffered great distress and hardship. Manuchihr's father believed he had to divorce his second wife and, again in line with custom, she left her baby with him, while he made provision for her upkeep and welfare. Mehri remembers with great affection Manuchihr's stepmother, who was so good to him and treated him as her own son such that Manuchihr often forgot that she was not his birth mother.

When the Shah decreed in 1925 that all births were to be registered and surnames issued, Manuchihr's eldest brother, who was living in Isfahan, took the surname Nádirí. Other members of the family should have been given the same surname, but when Manuchihr's father went to register the rest of the family, the official ignored the fact that the whole point of issuing surnames was so that family names would be established. He refused to allow the name 'Nádirí' to be given to them on the grounds that enough people were already called that and thus another name had to be chosen. His father asked for 'Farzaneh' but that also was refused, so he had to settle for 'Farzaneh-Moayyad'. Thus when Manuchihr was born in 1927 and his father went to register the birth of his new son, the baby had a name that was different from that of his eldest brother but was perhaps lucky in that he at least had the same name as his parents and most of his siblings.

Manuchihr was a good student at school and excelled at languages. He spoke Farsi perfectly, of course, and was also fluent in Turkish, French and English. He had a good grasp of Arabic and spoke some Italian. He also wrote poetry. One of his poems was to Mehrangiz, each line starting with a letter of her name.

One of the things he enjoyed doing most was writing a regular newspaper column on the appreciation of poetry and literature. The column, headed with his photograph, was written when he was based in Qazvin. He had also a great appreciation of music, although he did not play an instrument himself.

After finishing his primary and high school education, Manuchihr went to the University of Abadan to study electrical engineering. His studies were interrupted when one of his older brothers asked for his help with a project in which he was involved. This brother was a university lecturer but also owned a major construction company. He had a contract to build a dam near Abadan but because of his university commitments he needed someone to oversee the project for him. Manuchihr took over from him and completed the dam in his absence. Immediately this project was completed, another one started, this time to improve the water supply to Tabriz. Manuchihr was not very happy in the environment in which he found himself. The industry was 'cut-throat', and the constant demand for bribes to get anything done was completely against his principles.

He had never finished his degree course because Abadan University was British-run, and when the Anglo-Iranian Oil Company was nationalized in 1951, that was the end of the university, at least at that time. Manuchihr tried a job in a cement factory for a while but was not really settled in that as a career, so he left to join a French company, building more dams in the north of Iran. His abilities, integrity and dedication to his job had begun to be noticed by this time. The next project was building the headquarters of the French–Iranian Bank of Credit.

It was while on that job that Manuchihr became fluent in French. The bank badly needed fluent French and English speakers, and he was offered a position dealing with human resources, public relations and personnel. When General de Gaulle visited Iran, Manuchihr was detailed to organize the visit and to accompany the General on his various travels. It was suggested that Manuchihr study banking formally. He completed the course with distinction and then moved into bank management, eventually becoming deputy head of the bank's central branch based in Tehran. Because he was so trusted, he was expected to do the auditing and was involved in many confidential business matters.

Manuchihr's patience and good humour were legendary. Perhaps the best illustration of these qualities is in Mehri's account of how he reacted on one occasion when they were out in the car.

Manuchihr was a good, experienced driver. When Mehri learned to drive she became a very nervous passenger, constantly telling him what to do: 'Look out!' 'Mind that!' 'Watch this!' He never complained, never reminded her how long he had been driving without her assistance, which might have been reasonable in the circumstances. The more experience of driving she had, the worse she became as a passenger. At the end of a long drive her muscles would be aching from the effort of using an imaginary brake pedal, her foot almost going through the floor with the effort. She would be stiff from holding herself tense, ready to take any evasive action which might never be necessary. The worst moment came when she actually made a grab for the wheel and tried to wrest control of the car from him.

On that occasion he spoke to her very calmly, very quietly, but very firmly.

'My dear, you are welcome to criticize my driving as much as you like; to offer me as much instruction as you feel I need. You are welcome to draw my attention to any hazard, however remote, you feel I might have missed; to offer me any help you feel I might need; but do not, ever, under any circumstances, try to take the wheel from me again.'

She never did – but keeping herself in check required a great deal of effort.

According to their younger son, Fardin, Manuchihr always dealt reasonably and fairly with any youthful misdemeanours. They were able to learn from their mistakes because he dealt with whatever they had done rationally and always kept his sense of humour, however trying they had been.

Manuchihr had a mischievous, almost childlike, sense of humour which was sometimes embarrassing to his children. Fardin recalled that on more than one occasion his father loosened all the tops of the salt cellars so that some unwary soul would be astonished to find a whole heap of salt on his plate. Fardin said that his father's sense of humour embarrassed him sometimes, but that as he gets older, he is astonished to find himself saying or doing things in a very similar way.

Occasionally, Manuchihr liked to cook for his family. He would shut himself in the kitchen and produce a speciality of his, a sort of biryani, but quite unlike the Indian dish of that name. It required a base of minced lamb, with lots of spices. He always refused to divulge the secret of this recipe, which became a family favourite and was much enjoyed by them all.

One of Manuchihr's pastimes, when he had any spare time, was needlework. An unusual choice perhaps, but apparently he enjoyed it very much. He used to work on canvases that were prepared with colour coding to show where each stitch should be placed, a sort of 'tapestry by numbers' kit. It was this sort of kit that he would work on when he was in prison, awaiting execution – a calming exercise for an active mind, no doubt.

In Tehran, Manuchihr's duties had included overseeing the construction of the bank's new headquarters, and the selecting and training of new staff. After he had been in Tehran for some years, he requested a transfer to the city of Qazvin as at that time there was a wish for Bahá'ís to move out of the capital into more rural areas.

His duties at this new post in Qazvin again included selecting and training staff. He also found time to train bank staff at Qazvin University. The family stayed there for about four years, during which time Manuchihr was very active in the Faith, being elected to the local spiritual assembly, a body that looks after the affairs of a local Bahá'í community. At this time, their younger son, Fardin, who was then 12, was sent to a German boarding school in Tehran, so that his education was not interrupted.

From Qazvin, Manuchihr was transferred to Shiraz,

the provincial capital of Fars. In Shiraz he was in charge of all the bank's branches in the province. Again, he was a very active Bahá'í, being an enthusiastic member of several local and national committees.

The family's move to Shiraz coincided with the start of the Islamic Revolution in 1979. They had been there for two and a half years when word reached the bank headquarters in Tehran that local clerics were speaking against Manuchihr in the mosques and at various gatherings. There were posters at local mosques and other places with his name and photograph openly displayed and details of his Bahá'í activities. His 'crimes' were reported as 'teaching the Bahá'í Faith' and 'being in charge of young Muslim staff at the bank'. The bank decided to investigate what was going on and sent a man, a French national, to Shiraz to verify the situation and to report back. The inspector not only wrote a glowing report about Manuchihr but by the time he left he had several Bahá'í books and contact numbers in France so that he could investigate the religion for himself. He also reported that the situation was very alarming.

Manuchihr received a telegram from the bank's board stating, 'For your own safety and [in light of] the value placed on you as an employee, move back to Tehran immediately.'

When the family left Shiraz, Manuchihr received a message from members of the local spiritual assembly in Qazvin, telling him not to return to that town because they genuinely feared his life would be in danger if he did.

By this time Bahá'ís were barred from holding any employment but the most menial. Companies were not allowed to employ Bahá'ís. Some who lost their jobs, and the pensions which should have gone with them, were even faced with the demand that they repay all previous salaries, which could have been for 20 years' employment or more. In the case of Manuchihr, the bank refused to terminate his employment, offering him instead early retirement after 18 years of loyal service.

6

Revolution

Life changed irrevocably for everyone in Iran in 1979. The consequences of a complete cataclysm in the affairs of the country affected all the people, to a greater or lesser degree. The ousting of the Shah by the supporters of the exiled Ayatollah Khomeini, and the return of the country to the control of the religious clerics, meant that nearly 60 years of efforts towards modernization were swept away. Two weeks after the Shah was forced to leave Iran and go into exile with his wife and family, Ayatollah Khomeini returned from his exile, which had lasted more than 14 years. Khomeini had been sent into exile for denouncing the Shah and his pro-western stance, going first to Turkey, then Iraq and finally France, from where he had been able to coordinate the actions of his followers that were to end in violent revolution.

In 1979, just after the revolution started, Mehrangiz and Manuchihr sent their two sons to the UK to continue their education. This had been planned for some time, and they saw no reason to change the plans because of the upheaval in Iran. At that time travel was not restricted for Bahá'ís and initially they had no difficulty sending money out of the country to support the boys. After the revolution, making contact by telephone became more difficult, and the boys also reported that their letters had often been interfered with. The postmen would apologize and say, 'It was opened in Iran.'

In August 1980 the younger of the two boys went back to Iran for a visit in connection with a property that Manuchihr had bought in Shiraz and wanted to transfer into his sons' names in view of the deteriorating situation. It was to be the last time he would see his own country. This visit, or the end of it, coincided with the disappearance of their aunt, Bahíyyih Nádirí. Manuchihr visited the UK sometime in 1979 or 1980 and was warned by friends in Oxford that it was too dangerous for him to return to Iran, urging him to stay and send for Mehri and Roshanak to join him.

When the Ayatollah Khomeini returned to Iran it was to a rapturous welcome. He wasted no time in making clear who was in charge. He denounced the remnants of the Shah's government as illegal and threatened to arrest all its members if they tried to continue in office, and to bring them before special courts. He appointed a new prime minister and began to implement his own vision of government. One month later he announced that there was no room for democracy in Iran. It was his intention that Iran be a theocracy, a religious government which would enforce strict observance of Islam. A week later, Iranian women chose International Women's Day to march to the Palace of Justice in Tehran demanding the right to dress as they pleased, under the slogan, 'Freedom not the Chador', braving the Ayatollah's wrath, but prepared to show their fear for the future under the new strict Islamic laws. Previously, women had been allowed education and careers, and at least one of the government ministers had been a woman, the Minister of Education. But now they faced the sort of repression that would allow them no role in society except at a domestic level, with no choices open to them, and completely subject to the rule of men. This was what they feared, with good reason, as they were soon to find out.

Soon after his return to Iran, Ayatollah Khomeini issued a fatwa – a ruling on a matter of Islamic law – ordering Jews, Christians, Zoroastrians and other religious minorities which pre-date Islam, to be treated well. This fatwa specifically excluded Bahá'ís and virtually declared 'open season' on the Bahá'í Faith. It was to be the start of a period of repression that was unprecedented and would include killings, torture, disappearances of individuals, imprisonment without charge; confiscation of property, destruction or confiscation of Bahá'í centres, holy places, cemeteries, hospitals; loss of jobs and pensions; Bahá'ís being denied passports and admission to further education, in some cases being denied any education at all. The list is endless.

In Shiraz, the house where in 1844 the Báb had declared His station to the first of His followers and which had become a sacred place of pilgrimage for Bahá'ís from around the world, and which had already suffered attacks and vandalism in the past and been lovingly restored, was bull-dozed out of existence. The Mosque of Mahdi was eventually built over the site, in an attempt to expunge the historical significance of the home. This completed what had been started under the Shah. Even the orange tree that had grown in the garden of the Báb was torn up. However, for years Bahá'í pilgrims had been carrying away the fruits of this tree and carefully nurturing the seeds. Orange trees grown from the Báb's tree are flourishing all over the world, so that one day seedlings from this tree will bloom again in the garden of the Báb, Deo volente, when the time is right.

The Bahá'í Faith has a unique way of organizing its affairs. Starting at the grassroots, each community elects nine members to administer it. These nine are elected from all Bahá'ís who are 21 years old and over, male or female. In these elections, everyone is a candidate but no one is allowed to offer themselves for election or to nominate others. It is a duty to elect those individuals who are thought to possess the right spiritual qualities for the job. If elected, it is the duty of those chosen to serve as well as possible, however unsuitable they might feel they are. Once elected, these nine people are known as the Local Spiritual Assembly (LSA) of the town or village. They hold office for one year and are responsible for the affairs of the community. All elections must take place in a prayerful atmosphere and by secret ballot.

Once a year, several communities in an area are called together to hold a unit convention to elect a delegate from amongst their members to attend a national convention. Again, all adult Bahá'ís 21 and over are candidates and again no electioneering is permitted. In a Bahá'í election, were anyone to say, 'vote for me', that person would be demonstrating his or her complete lack of the spiritual qualities looked for in a suitable candidate.

The next step in the process is the national convention, where the delegates vote to elect nine members of the National Spiritual Assembly (or NSA), the body which is responsible for overseeing Bahá'í affairs in the country. All adult Bahá'ís in the country are eligible for election. This body is re-elected every year.

One of the functions of every National Assembly throughout the world is to attend as delegates the international convention which elects the Universal House of Justice, the body guiding the worldwide Bahá'í community. The international convention takes place every five years and those not able to attend send postal ballots. When electing the Universal House of Justice, the delegates can choose from the worldwide community of male believers, all of whom are considered candidates. It is an amazing spectacle to see representatives of almost every nation on earth, in their national costumes if they have such a thing, all gathered together to elect the House of Justice. It truly represents the unity of mankind that the Bahá'í Faith teaches. The term of those elected to the Universal House of Justice is five years, and they may be elected to serve further terms. They give up their homes and their employment to spend years of their lives in service to their fellow Bahá'ís for little more than basic living expenses, and count it an honour to serve.

If the Local and the National Spiritual Assemblies are not allowed to operate in a particular part of the world, the worldwide community is deprived of their spiritual input and experience.

After the revolution, the administration of the Faith

in Iran came under direct and systematic attack. First, individuals serving on the National Assembly and Local Assemblies were targeted, along with other influential Bahá'ís. The list of officially-sanctioned killings and executions based on trumped-up charges grew longer and longer.

In November 1979 the secretary of the National Spiritual Assembly of Iran was kidnapped and never seen again, presumed dead. In August 1980 Manuchihr's sister-in-law, Mrs Bahíyyih Nádirí, 'disappeared' along with all other eight members of the National Spiritual Assembly and two others, when they were abducted by armed men from a private home. It is presumed they were all killed but no one ever admitted responsibility. Their families do not know what happened to them or where their bodies are.

It soon became obvious that the Revolutionary Government had systematically arrested the most prominent Bahá'ís, those who were very active in the administration, Local and National Assembly officeholders, and those who were very wealthy or were thought to be most influential. Any means were to be used to 'persuade' them to recant, to declare that their having embraced the Bahá'í Faith was a mistake and that they were willing, nay, eager, to recant their religion. These means included enticement, threats, torture and ultimately, if those did not work, the Bahá'ís were executed, hence the long list of executions.

By 1980 a pattern was clearly emerging: the Bahá'í administration at both national and local levels was being targeted. Three members of the Local Spiritual Assembly in Tabriz were executed in July 1980. Then there were five in Yazd in September of the same year and seven members of the Local Spiritual Assembly of Hamadan in June 1981. Another eight Local Assembly members were executed in Tabriz in July that year. One can only imagine with what trepidation the ones chosen to replace their executed comrades would valiantly take their places, but they did.

In December 1981 eight of the National Spiritual Assembly members elected to replace those abducted the year before were executed. Only a week later six members of the Local Spiritual Assembly of Tehran were also lost by execution. The new members of the National Spiritual Assembly were elected in 1982.

After this, in August 1983, the Iranian Attorney General issued an order forbidding participation in any Bahá'í administrative activity, making service on a Bahá'í institution a criminal offence. In response, the National Spiritual Assembly issued a statement outlining all the abuses the Bahá'ís had suffered and calling for the restoration of their rights. As a final act, the National Assembly disbanded itself and all the Local Spiritual Assemblies in the country, in obedience to their government.

When the National Spiritual Assembly and Local Spiritual Assemblies were obliged to stop all their activities, the authorities may have assumed that these bodies would simply go underground and try to continue the work. However, obedience to the government of one's country is an important tenet of the Bahá'í Faith, so the Bahá'ís obeyed and disbanded all their administrative bodies. Various individuals continued to keep the friends in contact with one another, passing on messages of hope and support, performing Bahá'í marriage services, recording births, marriages and deaths, and collating information about what the people were enduring. Just as it had been before the revolution, under the new regime Bahá'í marriages were not recognized as legal. Anyone performing the marriage, or the couple being married, could be killed on the grounds that they were condoning 'prostitution'. This was deeply insulting to a people who do not indulge in sex outside marriage and whose religion emphasises the importance of marriage as the stable bedrock of a civilized society.

Manuchihr was one of the people trying to keep up the spirits of his fellows, and at the same time keep within the new laws that were making life difficult for them all. When Mehri tried to warn her husband of the dangers of what he was doing, as even the possession of any information about the followers of the Faith would be held to be incriminating, he said, 'Others are doing far more than I am. It embarrasses me that I am not doing enough.'

7

Arrested

Manuchihr had always been very active within the Baháʼí community but by the late seventies, even before the revolution started, he began to find even more ways open to him to increase his activities. There was so much to be done, he seemed to find new energy. It was as if he had a new lease of life, if that were possible. He increased his involvement at local and national levels. If Mehri warned him, he replied, 'Others are risking their lives and making tremendous sacrifices.'

He was proud to do what he perceived to be the little that he could. He knew the dangers he faced but was prepared to accept whatever happened to him as a small price to pay for serving the Cause of God to the betterment of all mankind.

On 1 May 1982 Manuchihr travelled to Qazvin on public transport. Mehri was uneasy about this journey and asked him not to go.

He replied confidently, 'I'll be finished by lunchtime!' and departed.

Despite the warnings he had received earlier, Manuchihr had persuaded himself that because his Baháʼí activities in Qazvin had all taken place before the revolution, he would not be in any danger there.

His reason for going to Qazvin was to make contact

with Bahá'ís. But no one was at home when he arrived: they had either been arrested or had fled. His task was to try to establish the truth of recently published 'recantations' but he did not find anyone who would admit to knowing anything about what was going on locally.

Manuchihr was waiting for a bus when a taxi with several men in it pulled up alongside him. He waved it away but was told to get in, they would make room for him. Since they were all heavily armed, he realized that he had no option but to obey. The driver pulled away sharply from the bus stop.

Manuchihr protested but was told, 'You have some questions to answer.'

He was driven to the Revolutionary Court, a building which he remembered as having once belonged to friends of his.

'When you have done, you will be free to leave.'

The other passengers were all Revolutionary Guards who had been cruising around looking for him or anyone else they were interested in. It seems that he had been caught purely by chance, when someone recognized him from a photograph which was in circulation.

At four o'clock in the afternoon Mehrangiz received a telephone call from the Office of the Revolutionary District Attorney telling her that Manuchihr had been arrested.

'We have some questions. If he answers, he can go home,' said the official, and gave Mehri the address where they were holding him. Mehri knew the address, it was an office building which had formerly belonged to family friends and fellow Bahá'ís.

It was not until two days later that Mehri was permitted to visit Manuchihr. He was brought up from the basement of the building surrounded by armed guards. They told her that his photo had been issued to the Revolutionary Guards, so he could have been arrested anywhere, at any time.

'If you persuade him to cooperate, the guards told her, 'he can go home with you to Tehran today.'

Manuchihr asked the guards if he could give Mehri a note he had written about some things he wanted her to take care of for him. They checked it carefully, then gave it to her. There were three items on the list:

1. I have bought a fridge, it is paid for. You don't need to pay for it when it is delivered.

2. Before you pack away my raincoat for the summer, make sure you get it dry-cleaned.

3. The ceiling in bathroom is leaking, might need fixing. Get Amir the builder to have a look at the plaster before it falls down.

The first item was obviously a red herring. Mehri knew Manuchihr had not bought a refrigerator because they had bought a new one when they moved from Shiraz to Tehran. The other two she would investigate when she got home. The raincoat puzzled her very much. She searched the pockets but found nothing. Then she noticed a small area of stitching on a seam which had been redone. After carefully unpicking it, she found a scrap of paper with directions to look in the ceiling for a box. 'Amir the builder' was not called 'Amir' and he was not a builder: he had served on the same local committees as Manuchihr. He came and carefully searched in the bathroom ceiling, which was wooden, not plaster. Before he found anything, Amir jokingly grumbled, 'This Manuchihr, always making jokes! He must think I have nothing better to do!'

It was very well hidden, but at last, behind a small panel which had been cut away and replaced so that it could be removed without too much difficulty, Amir found a box which contained lists of Bahá'ís, marriage certificates, birth and death certificates, a small sum of money belonging to the LSA, some certified cheques for the National Spiritual Assembly, various administrative records and other papers, all totally innocent, but lethal in the wrong hands.

There was also an account of tortures and executions in Hamadan, the only record in existence at that time. There had been a massive public demonstration in Hamadan in support of seven Bahá'ís who had been brutally tortured and killed there. Everyone, Muslim and Bahá'í alike, had been able to see for themselves the state of the bodies and the tortures that had been inflicted on these people. The condemnation of the authorities grew louder as the procession following the funeral to the cemetery became well over a mile long, as more and more of the local populace left their homes and businesses to join the throng. They listened with respect to the prayer for the dead and joined in the chanting of the repetitive parts of the Bahá'í text.

The wife of one of the dead men gave a moving speech about the seven who had died, concluding: 'These seven innocent men have shed their blood so that the hearts of all men everywhere can be freed from all hatred and enmity.'

Her words were well received and both Muslim and Bahá'í listeners were deeply touched. The event very much upset the authorities, who really did not want the details to be made public.

Also in the box found by Amir were lists of charges brought against individuals. All this would have to be disposed of or found a safer hiding place. Just possessing such records could land any of the Bahá'ís in prison. Indeed, Amir was later to suffer the same fate as Manuchihr.

Manuchihr had always been very active as a member of the Bahá'í Faith, serving on Local Spiritual Assemblies, sometimes as chairman or secretary. Every Tuesday evening, for many years, wherever they were living, he and Mehri had held 'firesides' in their home, informal meetings which anyone wanting to investigate the Faith could attend if invited. He would rise at dawn every day for prayers and had formed the habit of trying to memorize as many prayers and writings of the Báb and Bahá'u'lláh as he could. He knew that Bahá'í books were being destroyed all over Iran and what is committed to memory stays with one for a lifetime. He was honoured when he was appointed an assistant to an Auxiliary

Board member and was pleased because it meant he would still have the time to serve on a Local or National Assembly. The Auxiliary Boards have been in existence since 1954. Their purpose is to protect and propagate the Faith. Their members are appointed, not elected, and are usually chosen for their individual special qualities. They have no power to make administrative decisions or judgements but offer advice and counsel when called upon. Like any other position in the Faith, the work is voluntary and unpaid.

Another of Manuchihr's tasks was to meet and talk to prisoners who had been released. Had their defence been successful? Had they been tortured? How were they coping now? It was important to establish who needed help and support.

On Mehri's next visit Manuchihr asked, 'Can I give some washing to my wife, please?'

It was only his vest and pants but he was actually trying to pass her a note but was frustrated by the guards inspecting the bundle. By chance, a special investigator from Qom who had been called in to interrogate Manuchihr was coming down the staircase above them just at that moment.

Manuchihr looked up and pointed at him saying, 'Look Mehri, this gentleman does me the honour of coming here every day from Qom, just to ask me questions!'

As all the guards looked upwards, he tossed Mehri a tiny, screwed-up pellet of paper, which she managed to catch and conceal. Her knees were quaking at that moment! On this tiny scrap of paper Manuchihr had carefully listed all the questions the interrogators had asked him because he believed it was vitally important to get as many of these details as possible on record for posterity to evaluate. Each of them knew Manuchihr was risking both their lives to get this information but it made no difference. By these means, and others, Manuchihr managed to collate invaluable information about all the others arrested and held prisoner, and all the questions asked.

Manuchihr was held in this house for nine days altogether. On 10 May he was sentenced to death; the date of his execution was to be 13 May. He was told to write his will, which was dated 13 May, the date of the will usually being the same date as the day of execution. He did not tell Mehri that he had been sentenced to death. The few friends who did know carefully conspired to keep it from her.

One lady told Mehri later, 'My husband knew your husband was to be executed, but he said he didn't want you to know, and we were praying it would not be carried out, so we did not tell you.'

Even after the sentence was passed Manuchihr was asked to recant, to deny his faith, to give them all the information they wanted, and if he did, everything – house, furniture, job, bank accounts and pension – would be restored to him. It would no doubt have been good propaganda for them if he had recanted but he stood firm.

Manuchihr was then transferred to a prison near Qazvin. Mehri was told that she could visit him every

Tuesday. He was held there for another two months, perhaps because they wanted to give him plenty of time to deny his faith and give them the result they wanted.

Visiting him one day, Mehri was worried because another prisoner, who had been released sometime before, had told her that mock executions were carried out every day, just to wear down the nerves and break the individual's resolve.

Manuchihr smiled and said, 'Oh, they joke with one sometimes. Last night I was taken for execution at one a.m., but here I am!'

During one visit, Mehri and her sister asked how he was.

He replied, 'I am fulfilling my lifelong ambition!'

'What ambition?' they asked him.

'Teaching the word of God!'

Something that was of more concern to Manuchihr at that time, however, concerned a conversation that Mehri herself told him about. She had had a visitor who told her that a National Spiritual Assembly member had told him, 'Recant and God will forgive you.'

Manuchihr did not believe this. He was very familiar with all the writings and laws of the Faith, and he knew that no National Assembly could change the law of God. To recant one's religion is not acceptable in the sight of God, whatever the religion. All through the ages, many brave individuals have been prepared to die rather than deny their faith, and the Bahá'í Faith is no different.

He asked Mehri to contact a particular member of the former National Spiritual Assembly, Mr Bashiri, who would be able to speak to other former members. As the Assembly could no longer meet, this took some time, but eventually Mr Bashiri met her at the house of Mehri's sister.

Mr Bashiri, who was subsequently to be executed himself, was adamant. 'Whoever said this, it is not so. It was probably put about by someone desperate to save their relatives. No credence is to be attached to it.'

At the next visit, Mehri was able to confirm for Manuchihr that his understanding of the laws was correct: no one was to recant. Manuchihr passed this on to the other prisoners, some of whom were obviously distressed and disappointed, their hopes dashed for no easy way out provided.

While in prison Manuchihr thought of everything but his own situation. He was very worried about his sons because the papers and documents taken from their house had included their educational records and details of the college they attended in Scotland. He had been told that if he did not cooperate and recant, they would be harmed.

Manuchihr was allowed to do his needlework when he was able to. He also wove a little raffia bookcase for Shana. In this way he kept himself occupied through the dreary hours of enforced inactivity.

Week by week, Mehri could see that he was losing weight. Once when she and her cousin were visiting him he was visibly in pain. His right thumb was crudely bandaged. When the cousin asked, 'How are you?', he became agitated and tried to hide the thumb, saying it was nothing much. He relaxed when she explained that she was asking about his chest complaint. Another prisoner later told Mehri that he had been tortured 'very badly'. It was believed that this was punishment because he had helped a fellow Bahá'í prisoner, a former member of the Local Spiritual Assembly, who was illiterate, by preparing his defence. It had been successful and the man was released.

Manuchihr was able to send out from prison his consent to the marriage of Farshid, his eldest son. A Bahá'í wishing to marry requires the consent of all living parents, including those who are not Bahá'ís. Mehri had passed on the message that Farshid was seeking their consent to his marriage to Rose and was able to tell him what she knew of her future daughter-in-law, explaining that Rose's family in Scotland had given their consent and were happy with her choice of husband.

The document that Manuchihr was permitted to give to Mehri reads: 'I say firstly I believe in God, and in the Bahá'í Faith marriage is very important, and I consent to this marriage.'

This message was allowed to be passed to Mehri by the very people who were doing everything possible to suppress the Faith and everything about it.

'He was such a special person,' Mehri says, 'always so brave and strong. I could not have believed that one day my husband would have to go through something like that. In all his life, since I met him, all the time I knew him, I do not remember him ever saying anything bad, or doing anything bad, towards anyone. He was never jealous of anyone. He never bore any grudges towards anyone. He always tried to help anyone he could. If anyone let him down he would say, "Maybe there is something I need to learn from this." He was always very generous and very loving. He thought of everyone but himself, always.'

Part Two

'. . . brings forth monsters'
Francisco José de Goya, 1746–1828

8

The Execution

It was about four o'clock in the morning of the 9th of July when Mehri and Shanna, after a restless, edgy night, decided to lie down and try to sleep a little. Fifteen minutes later, Mehri awoke with a start from a vivid dream. In her dream she had been to the prison for a visit but she was puzzled. She was not searched. There was none of the usual unpleasant 'rigmarole', as she describes it, before she was allowed in. The prison was not the usual dark, dingy, threatening place she knew. She went into a huge open space that was sunny and light. She saw Manuchihr in the distance. He was standing very upright, looking much as she was used to seeing him at home, his hands behind his back, and very relaxed, as if out for his usual evening stroll.

'Why is it so different here now?' she asked him.

His reply seemed rather strange. 'Since the visits have become three at a time now, things are different.'

As they strolled along holding hands, they passed a mound of reddish earth and they seated themselves there.

Mehri said to him, 'While you were in prison we knew things were very difficult for you. I have tried to hide from you how difficult we are finding things without you. Now it is like this, I feel I can tell you how hard it really is for us.'

Manuchihr became distressed and walked away into a little shed. Mehri followed him, feeling ashamed and embarrassed for troubling him. There were several other men inside the shed, which was like a caravan inside.

She asked him, 'Who are these other people? Are they the ones you mentioned?'

'No,' he said, 'I do not know them.'

At this point Mehri looked at her watch, as visiting time was usually strictly limited.

'I didn't realize what time it is,' she said. 'They will come and throw me out any minute now.'

'No, time does not matter now,' Manuchihr replied. 'Now you can see me at any time you wish.'

Mehrangiz was so delighted that she began to hug and kiss him. Then she woke up. She was so affected by this vivid dream that she felt sure something must have happened.

By seven o'clock she was no longer able to contain herself and telephoned her cousin to tell her about the dream and what she thought it might signify. Her cousin told her sister about it and they were agreed that it probably indicated something was very wrong.

Mehri was so unsettled by this that she told other people about it. There was no information from the authorities. When someone went to the prison to ask if they could see Manuchihr, they were turned away with the brusque comment to come only on the proper visiting day.

It was one o'clock a.m. on Saturday the tenth of July when Mehri received a telephone call from a woman she knew. The woman was very distressed. She had extremely bad news to impart. Three Bahá'í men had been executed early the previous day, or late on the night of Thursday the 8th. One was Manuchihr and another was the lady's brother-in-law. The third was another friend known to both of them. Mehri and Shanna's shock and distress need not be described. It was shared by all their relatives, friends and neighbours.

Later that morning Mehri went to Qazvin to meet the wives of the other men executed at the same time. The Bahá'í cemetery had been destroyed some time before these events and there was at that time no approved place for their dead to be interred, so it was a major problem. Arrangements were already in hand for the funerals but first they would have to find out if the Revolutionary Court would release the bodies. If permission was refused, then the bodies would be flung into a mass grave in a barren field reserved for infidels and the families could not expect to be told where that was. At least the families knew that their relatives were dead. So many people simply 'disappeared' into the system, their fate never disclosed and the authorities denying all knowledge of what had happened to them.

When Mehri went to the Revolutionary Court, she discovered that the waiting area was just like the inside of the 'caravan' in her dream. There had also been another three men executed at the same time but, as Manuchihr had 'told' her, these three were 'not known to us'. It was the mother of one of these young men who had been notified of her son's death. When she went to

the mortuary, she recognized some of the other dead as
Bahá'ís. She then told this to a Bahá'í who lived near her,
and the word was passed on. None of the Bahá'í families
were officially told of the deaths.

Mehri was given her husband's property, such as it was,
but it included his will, the craftwork and embroidery
which had kept him so serenely occupied. The hand-
written will had a note added: 'Sent for execution 9.55
p.m. in Qazvin on 8th July 1982' and a phone number,
with the words, 'Kindly inform my wife on this number'.
The full text of this document, dated 13 May 1982, reads:

Last Will and Testament

In the name of God, the Glory of the All Glorious.

After acknowledging the Oneness of God, I give
thanks to Him for He has favoured me till this
moment to write these words as my last will, for doing
so is an obligation and obedience to the Lord's com-
mandments.

I declare that I am in good health, physically and
mentally.

After confessing to my belief in the Báb as the
Forerunner; in the Ancient Beauty, Bahá'u'lláh, may
His praise be glorified, as the Manifestation of God
and fulfilment of all the past religions; in 'Abdu'l-Bahá
as the Interpreter and the Centre of the Covenant; in
Shoghi Rabbani as the only Guardian of the Cause
of God; and declaring my obedience to the infallible
institution, the Universal House of Justice, and my

unconditional acceptance of all the laws and ordi-
nances of the Baháʼí Faith, I write these words as my
last will and I declare that I deny the accusations made
about me and by which they are executing me.

At these ending moments I testify to my complete
innocence and since I regard this as the will of God, I
request my family not to be perturbed by this incident
and leave all their affairs to God, for He doeth what He
willeth, and trust in Him at all times.

Give my regards to all the friends and relatives. I
wish you all the best of health.

Signed: Manuchihr Farzaneh-Moayyad

This document, with the note he had made as to the time
of his execution, is annotated 'This is an exact copy' by
the prison, as the original was taken away from Mehri's
house during a search some time later, and she was only
to regain possession of the copy after she had been in
prison and was facing execution herself. But more of that
later.

She heard afterwards from other prisoners that
Manuchihr's calm and determination were incredible,
that he seemed pleased and happy, 'as if going to meet
friends'. He waved to other prisoners and walked firmly
with the guards. He had asked to have his hands untied
so that he could add the note to his will.

In addition to the will, Mehri was given a death certificate issued by the prison authorities. It gives the date,
his name and his place of birth but 'Cause of Death' is left
blank. Mehri was also allowed to copy out the charges

against him but the original was retained by the authorities. The Bahá'ís were trying to gather as much information as possible as to what was being done to them, so any scrap of information was potentially important.

The charges against Manuchihr were set out thus:

1. Manuchihr's name and birth certificate number, issued in Tehran. Was 'Managing Director' of National Spiritual Assembly of Bahá'ís

2. Very active member of Bahá'í committees in various cities

3. Very active member of Bahá'í Assemblies in different cities

4. Spymaster who sent spies to various locations to gather geographical and economic information and sending on this information to Israel

5. Misleading and trying to convert Muslim youth to Bahá'í Faith

6. Sending funds to Israel and direct contact with the Israeli government

Mehri painstakingly made a careful copy of this 'charge sheet' and had it verified as an authorized copy. She left the original behind as instructed.

Manuchihr's answers are not recorded, but Mehri

remembered everything he told her when he was first arrested.

- His answer to the first charge was that there is no such office as 'managing director' of any National Spiritual Assembly.

- He freely admitted charges two and three.

- In answer to the fourth charge, he told them that the only information sent to the World Centre concerned the plight of members of the Bahá'í Faith.

- Charge five was firmly refuted. He told them it is against the principles of the Faith to try to convert anyone and that individuals must investigate and decide for themselves which spiritual path to follow.

- Regarding charge six, Mehri has no recollection of him having to send funds to the World Centre, and he was never a National Treasurer.

Since the Bahá'ís were able to convince the prison authorities that proper arrangements had been made for the burials of the three men, the bodies were then released and they were even allowed the use of an old hearse to transport them the 30 miles from Qazvin to the field which was to be their last resting place. This field belonged to a Bahá'í farmer and its red soil was as Mehri had seen it in her dream.

Two of the bodies were already bloated in the early stages of decomposition and the smell was most unpleasant. Manuchihr was not in the same state. This was puzzling at first, but it was thought that the prison authorities might be mistaken about when they had all been killed, and that the other two had died a day or two before him. They were aware that the air-conditioning system in the mortuary had been deliberately turned off in order to hasten the process of decomposition but the family simply accepted it as yet another facet of official vindictiveness towards the Bahá'ís.

About 200 people risked their lives by attending the funeral. It was amazing how quickly the news had spread and how many came prepared to help with the practicalities, digging the graves and preparing the bodies. The Bahá'í Faith has no clergy and few rituals, so anyone can help as needed. There is one certain prayer to be said at a funeral, indeed this prayer is the funeral service, and as long as this is done, that is sufficient, although any other prayers and readings can be included as one wishes.

When the earth was replaced over the graves, a mound was left exactly as Mehri had seen it in the dream. She sat down on this mound and wept as she spoke to her beloved husband.

'Oh, Manuchihr, the last time I saw you, we sat here together. Now I sit here alone and you are gone from this world. How will I live without you?'

Then she remembered the message he had once sent her from prison: 'Be brave and accept because everything comes from God.'

After the funeral was over, Mehri determined to go back to the court and confront the official who was responsible for what was done in the mortuary. The state of the bodies, and the stench, had upset her very much. It seemed a very unpleasant thing for the authorities to condone, and she was resolved to try and do something about it. She returned to the court building and asked to speak to the official who had allowed her to copy the charges against her husband.

'In my religion,' she told him, 'when a person dies it does not matter what happens to the body. We are not bound by superstitions. But by allowing this (the turning off of the air conditioning), you cause distress and create a risk of infection for your staff and the public.' He agreed with her and said he had not realized what was happening. He sent a message to the mortuary staff telling them that the practice must cease immediately because it was a health hazard. He courteously thanked Mehri for bringing it to his attention.

This seems like any reasonable, civil exchange between two adults, but when one considers the considerable power over ordinary citizens wielded by this official and the regime he represented, to confront him in this way really was a remarkable act of courage on Mehri's part.

The officer recognized Mehri's family name from the official documents and asked her, 'Do you know Dr Ṣamadání?'

She replied, 'Yes, he is my brother!'

It transpired that this man had called for Dr Ṣamadání to attend his mother when the local doctors had given her up for dead. Dr Ṣamadání and his brother, a pharmacist, had treated her and had sat all night watching over her as she lay in a coma. She survived and her son was as grateful to the man who saved her as any loving son should be. In his gratitude he told Mehrangiz that they would remove some of the tenants from the house that had been confiscated and which was in the names of Farshid and Fardin so that Mehri and Shanna, and her sons when they returned, could live in a couple of rooms there.

Back in Tehran, the house was full of people when the telephone rang. It was her younger son, Fardin, from Scotland. She had not yet been able to bring herself to face the ordeal of contacting her sons and telling them the awful news, but he was crying as he asked, 'What has happened to Dad?'

'How did you know? she asked him. 'Who has told you?'

He explained that he had had a dream three nights before and knew instinctively that something dreadful had happened. His brother also shared these feelings of dread and both were anxiously waiting for news. They were devastated by what she had to tell them and both of them wanted to return to Iran to be with her and their sister. They felt the helpless guilt of being safe and secure in another country while such terrible things happened in their own. They would pack their bags and be ready to return as soon as she gave them the word.

Mehri was terrified at the thought of what would happen to them if they did return and was desperate to persuade them not to. Eventually she was able to convince them that their father would not want them to put themselves in such jeopardy, and that the worry would actually make her situation harder. She reminded them that this was not the first such death in their family but they should pray that it would be the last. Whatever happened must be accepted as the will of God.

In August 1980, the wife of Manuchihr's eldest brother, Mrs Bahíyyih Nádirí, was arrested, along with her eight fellow members of the National Spiritual Assembly of Iran, and two other Bahá'ís. They had simply 'disappeared' and were never heard of again. She was Shanna's most loved aunt and she missed her dreadfully.

Fardin had made what was to be his last visit back to Iran at that time and he remembers that on his last evening before his return to the UK his aunt hosted a dinner party for all the family. One of his cousins was a talented musician and gave an impromptu piano recital. Someone made a tape recording of this for Fardin to take away with him. When the cousin had finished playing, the tape was forgotten and left running, and he can still hear all the voices of his family, including his father, from that happy occasion. It was perhaps the last time any of them were to be truly happy. Bahíyyih Nádirí disappeared the very next day.

Manuchihr, Mehri and Shanna were staying with her and her husband. They went with Fardin to the airport early in the morning to see him off. When they got back to the house, Mrs Nádirí left to attend a National Assembly meeting, saying, 'Look after yourselves for a while, maybe get some sleep.'

A phone call later in the day told them that all nine members of the Assembly, and two visiting Board members, had been kidnapped. There was no official statement confirming that these people had been arrested. The families were never told what had happened to them. They were simply never seen again, alive or dead.

The nine people who replaced them as members of the National Assembly were arrested and executed in December 1981. These 1981 deaths were discovered by chance, as once again the families were not notified and the authorities denied all knowledge of this 'incident'. The membership of the National and Local Spiritual Assemblies continued steadfastly being replaced until the Revolutionary Government banned all Bahá'í administrative institutions. Then, because their Faith requires its followers to be obedient to the government of whichever country they reside in, the entire administration was disbanded by the Bahá'ís. No one has ever been held to account for, or has explained what happened to Mrs Nádirí and her fellow National Assembly members and the others.

Another relative, a writer who was married to Manuchihr's niece, was also executed by the Revolutionary Government.

9

. . . and Afterwards

In Tehran, after the execution, there was no peace at all for his grieving widow and daughter. The Revolutionary Guards visited almost daily, asking endless questions about Manuchihr's brothers, and about business interests or property any of them might have. They would 'confiscate' anything that appealed to them, and it was during one of these visits that one of them took Shanna's jewellery, a little gold chain and an amethyst ring. Inexplicably, they also took away the tiny little sample of the red soil from Manuchihr's grave. This was of no value to anyone but his grieving family, and can only have been intended to add to their distress.

They were checking up generally, always trying to find any links with prominent politicians from the time of the Shah, such links having been proclaimed a criminal offence. Since Bahá'ís are not allowed to involve themselves in politics, there was very little likelihood of any of them being connected with political figures. There is a popular misconception in Iran that because Bahá'ís were allowed jobs under the regime of the Shah, they were in fact supported by him. Nothing could be further from the truth. They were simply good, reliable, educated, trustworthy employees, and the Shah recognized and exploited that. Any appeals to him about the gross excesses of violence towards fellow Bahá'ís, for instance, fell on deaf ears.

After the funeral, Mehrangiz kept Manuchihr's blood-stained clothes because it was thought that, like the wills and the lists of 'charges' brought against the Bahá'ís, the mute evidence of these garments might eventually be useful in establishing what happened to those executed, if ever reason and stability were to be established in the country at some point in the future, when it might be possible to bring those responsible to justice. In 1925 when Reza Shah seized power and tried to modernize the country, he had overseen the creation of a judiciary, under a Minister of Justice, with courts and judges and lawyers. Until that time, justice, like education, had been in the hands of the mullás and the religious courts. The new Civil Code, which was prepared by a group which included an expert from France and was influenced by the civil codes of Europe, remained the basis of the legal system until the revolution in 1979. Justice became summary after the revolution but the basis on which to build a modern judiciary at some time in the future still remains.

Keeping Manuchihr's clothes was a very dangerous thing to do and would eventually lead to Mehri's own arrest. She had already sent the tapestry Manuchihr had made in the prison cell, his will and the list of charges against him to her sons in the UK for safekeeping, but could not bring herself to send them the clothes. She thought it would be just too painful and shocking for them to receive such grisly items.

After Manuchihr's death, their house in Tehran was

confiscated and so was the house in Qazvin that was in the names of Farshid and Fardin, as all property of executed prisoners was claimed by the government. Mehri had great financial difficulties and it became almost impossible for her to get money from any source. The children had accounts at the bank in Shiraz. When the staff there found out what had happened to Manuchihr they were all very upset; most of them were in tears. Some of them brought little gifts to Mehri to express their sorrow. When she tried to draw money out of the children's accounts, the bank checked their lists. A new 'black list' of accounts that were not allowed to be accessed had been issued that very day, and of course all their names were on it. The staff decided to backdate Mehri's request to the day before and allowed her to withdraw all the money in Shanna's account. For some internal reason they were unable to let her access Farshid and Fardin's accounts but at least she now had some funds to keep her going.

Some little time after the execution she was asked to attend a meeting in Tehran with the Iranian who was now the manager of the bank where Manuchihr had been employed. During the course of this meeting she was told that if she would convert to Islam and totally renounce her Faith, then his life insurance, bank account, the pensionable part of his salary, and all the properties and goods that had been confiscated would be restored to her. She refused to even consider such a thing. She was then told that she must fill in a form to say that she had rejected this offer and then sign it.

She was asked a number of questions, starting with her name and date of birth. She was then asked her Bahá'í registration number. Mehri explained that she no longer had a Bahá'í registration number as her marriage certificate and registration card were destroyed when the Bahá'í Centre in Tehran was attacked in 1955.

'Have you been to Israel?'

She answered, 'How could I travel with a young family?'

'Are you one of THOSE people?

Mehri asked, 'What does this mean, please? What people?'

'Are you a Bahá'í?'

'Oh, yes,' she replied. 'I am one of THOSE.' And she wrote I AM A BAHÁ'Í on the form.

'Are you a widow?'

She wrote, 'I do not feel that I am a widow. Always I feel that my husband is beside me.

After that she was asked again, 'You are a Bahá'í then?'

When she firmly answered, 'Yes!' she was shown out of the office, to face destitution, as far as they were concerned. This was the bank that had valued Manuchihr so highly when he was their employee, that had trusted him for all the years he had served them to the very best of his abilities, that been so concerned for his safety they had ordered him back to Tehran from Qazvin when his life was in danger, the bank that had allowed him to retire rather than sack him. But times, and personnel, had changed.

Many months later Mehri had an unwelcome visitor at her home in Qazvin. Another employee of the bank, a man who had given 'evidence' against Manuchihr at his trial, tried to see her. It was probably true that this man had been bribed with goods and money to testify against Manuchihr. He had given 'evidence' that Manuchihr had used bank time to teach his religion to young Muslim employees who were under his tuition at the time. This man was only a poorly-paid cleaner in the bank, so it was highly unlikely that he would ever have been present when Manuchihr was giving staff instructions, and in any case it would have been against all Manuchihr's principles to tell anyone anything about his religion at such times. He was far too conscientious to do that. Had anyone shown any interest in his religion, he would simply have invited him to attend the next 'fireside' meeting at his home, and carried on with the work of the bank in which they were engaged. That was always his way, as anyone who really knew him could have testified.

Immediately after the trial, another employee had said to this man, 'How could you do that? You are wearing the suit Mr Farzaneh-Moayyad gave you! And he also helped you with money, more than once. I know because you told me!'

When this man tried to see Mehrangiz she would not let him into her house. He had had an accident soon after the trial and, being very superstitious, had convinced himself that it was God's punishment for his perjury against a man like Manuchihr. On this occasion he tried to grovel at Mehri's feet, trying to kiss her hands and feet, seeking her forgiveness. In fear and revulsion she told him to go away.

10

The Woman on the Bus

It started out as an ordinary day. Mehri cannot remember where she was going, or what she had intended to do, only that she set out to go somewhere on a bus, probably on some domestic errand. Roshanak must have been at school, for Mehri was alone. If Shanna had been with her, the encounter might not have happened and she could have been spared the knowledge that will torment her for the rest of her life.

She had climbed aboard the bus and found a seat when suddenly a woman who once before had tried to speak to her was beside her. The strange woman was with her husband but she sent him to sit by himself at the back of the bus, telling him that she would sit here, 'with this lady'. Mehri was trapped.

She had not wanted to get into conversation with this stranger and on the previous occasion had managed to evade her, pleading that she had no time to stop and chat. That first time had been just after the death of her husband, when Mehri had thought she might be someone who simply wanted to offer her condolences, maybe an ex-colleague or a business acquaintance. Instinctively, Mehri had recoiled from entering into any conversation with this stranger, especially when, at the first chance meeting, the woman had said she had information about the death of Mr Moayyad. Now she was here, beside her, and Mehri could not escape. What the woman had to say would leave her totally devastated.

Mehri had accepted that her beloved husband was dead. She knew that he had been tortured before his execution. These stark realities had come to seem almost of lesser importance beside his serenity and peace of mind, his faith and his trust in God, which had become as a legacy for Mehri and his children. This was a man who, facing execution, had refused to save himself by denying his religion, and instead had resolutely accepted his fate. This was a man who, in such circumstances, had been able to occupy himself peacefully with beautiful needlework, one a tapestry picture of roses, a photographed copy of which hangs in Mehri's home today, and with doing his best to let his family know how much he loved and cared for them all and wanted them to be happy. Astonishingly, his original needlework, which was completed in the prison cell and which is now in the Bahá'í World Centre, had been handed to Mehrangiz along with his other effects, including the scrap of paper on which he had scribbled his will.

Now here was this woman, explaining that she was employed in some capacity – a nurse, or an orderly perhaps – in the hospital attached to the mortuary where the bodies of executed prisoners were kept until released to the families for burial, and it was there that she had seen Mehri and remembered her. At the funeral of Manuchihr and the two other Bahá'í men executed at the same time, it was clear that not all the bodies were in the same state.

Two were already decomposing, Manuchihr's body was not. It is a requirement under Islamic law that a body must be buried as soon as possible after death – most burials take place within 24 hours or at most three days. In hot desert countries this makes a great deal of sense on hygiene grounds alone. To this has accrued a belief, in some Islamic communities, that unless a body is buried before decomposition sets in, then the soul cannot ascend to heaven. In the prison system it is not always possible to adhere to general principle of swift burial. These bodies were in such a bad state because the air-conditioning system in the mortuary had been deliberately turned off, in an attempt to ensure that these Bahá'í souls could never ascend to heaven. Mehri had already told the man responsible what she thought of such a practice, saying it created a health hazard for the staff, and he had promised it would not be allowed to happen again. The different states of the three bodies had puzzled everyone involved with the funeral but it was supposed that they had simply been killed at different times. Now this woman was to make it terribly clear to Mehri why the body of Manuchihr had not been affected.

The usual method of execution used in these cases is either hanging, or a bullet in the back of the head, like common criminals. All these three had been shot. The two men executed at the same time as Manuchihr had both been shot in the head, and for them death must have been instantaneous. For some unknown reason, Manuchihr had not. The executioner had chosen instead to shoot him in the stomach. No merciful bullet to the head had followed. After being shot, his body had been carelessly dragged from the execution place for some distance, over thorny, rough ground. This was clearly demonstrated by the state of his clothes and the lacerations to his limbs and body. Delivered to the mortuary from the execution ground, he had been left to slowly bleed to death. The third and fourth fingers on one hand had been removed in an attempt to hide the signs of earlier torture. Whether this was done before or after the execution is not known. There was also an awful wound in his nose. Mehri was aware of all these details, of course. What she was unaware of was how long it had taken him to die. Now this woman, whatever her motive might be, was trying to make it brutally clear to her that he had not been dead when delivered to the mortuary. This was the reason why his body was in such a different state from the other two victims.

Through the long hours while the woman was on duty, it had been clearly seen that Manuchihr was still alive, biting his lower lip as if conscious of pain, and still trying to move the mutilated hand. The staff were all too terrified to dare to do anything to alleviate his suffering. Some time before this happened, the woman explained to Mehrangiz, there had been a similar case involving a young boy, who had also been sent for execution but was not dead on arrival at the mortuary. On that occasion, the staff had tried to help the victim, apparently a member of the Mujahaddin. When their efforts were discovered, all the personnel on duty at that time had themselves been executed. Whether this was true or not is not known, but it was believed to be true. Perhaps understandably, no one had been prepared to risk their own life to help the dying Manuchihr. The thought of her beloved husband dying slowly, in such pain, alone and abandoned, without help or comfort from anyone, was almost too much for Mehrangiz to bear. She knew that he had chosen to die rather than compromise his beliefs, but it would undoubtedly have been easier to know that a single shot had ended his life instantly. Having unburdened herself in this way, the woman, whose name she never knew, patted her hand in sympathy and blithely went to join her own husband. Mehri never saw her again.

The shock of Manuchihr's execution had a devastating effect on Mehrangiz, both physically and mentally. The gynaecological problems that had preceded the births of her three children had perhaps never been resolved, although opinions differ as to whether there could actually be any connection between her condition at the time of her several miscarriages and the state into which she fell after such a shock. It is always difficult to discuss 'women's problems', particularly for a naturally reticent lady who does not find it easy or comfortable to expose such very personal matters. Suffice to say that almost immediately after her husband's death she began to lose blood very heavily and went on to do so almost continuously for nearly eight months, until she was operated on. Any woman in that situation soon becomes severely anaemic and very weak indeed. Ordinary life becomes almost impossible. A walk to the shops, however conveniently close by they might be, soon becomes an expedition too far, and she is forced to become housebound, dependent on family or friends for the basic necessities of life.

The shocking details of Manuchihr's death, so callously disclosed to her by the woman on the bus, made Mehri's condition very much worse. It would have been easy for her to slide into a chronic depression, trying to live with such knowledge, but it was always her need to remain spiritually strong that came to the rescue. As always, she sought solace in prayer.

The Bahá'í doctor Mehri consulted eventually decided that surgery was the only option available. She urgently needed a hysterectomy, the removal of the womb, to stop the bleeding and save her life. Unfortunately, the Iran–Iraq war was raging, and the doctor she trusted was sent to the war zone before he could operate. Now her only option would have to be a Muslim surgeon in a Muslim hospital, where it was possible she might be turned away, on the grounds of her being a Bahá'í. The prospect frightened her, but she knew she must try to go through with it because she was getting weaker with each day that passed. The Bahá'í hospital in Tehran had been taken over by the Revolutionary Government sometime in 1980, and all Bahá'í personnel had been dismissed. All records and documents had been confiscated and there was now no place where Mehri could definitely go and would feel safe.

Normally, a patient in Mehri's situation would expect to be admitted to hospital two or three days before the surgery was scheduled so that she could be given a large blood transfusion in preparation for the operation.

Blood would also be given during the surgery and a top-up afterwards. This should be routine in such cases. However, Mehri was told that she would not be given a blood transfusion before the surgery as 'she was too weak to stand it'. The weakness was precisely why a transfusion was desperately needed. It could simply be that the bulk of blood and plasma supplies were diverted to the frontline of course, but one wonders. She was then told that because of the war, anaesthetics were also in such short supply that it was not possible to give her a general anaesthetic. Instead, they could only give her a local anaesthetic, an epidural. An epidural is an injection of anaesthetic into the epidural space around the spinal cord. This was not usually used for major surgery at that time. When Mehri realized that this had had little or no effect, and protested that this was the case, the surgeon went ahead anyway. She underwent this major operation with almost no pain relief whatsoever. The trauma can scarcely be imagined.

Very aware that if she prayed it would upset the staff attending her by reminding them that she was a Bahá'í, she resorted instead to reciting a sort of mantra to sustain herself throughout this ordeal. In translation from Farsi it went something like this: 'I am here. In a proper hospital. With proper doctors. Manuchihr had to suffer everything that was done to him without any help, his nose, his thumb, his fingers, his stomach. How could he bear it? What must he have suffered? If he had to stand all that, then I can bear this, which is being done to make me better.' She thought that she was saying all this to herself but she was actually repeating it aloud, over and over again. Afterwards a nurse told her what she had been saying. She realized later that throughout this ordeal she had clenched her fists so tightly that the fingernails had cut into the palms of her hands.

Recovering from such a traumatic experience was always going to be slow and difficult. A quiet, peaceful period of convalescence was what she really needed. Instead, she found that the Revolutionary Guards were even more intrusive, visiting almost daily, at any hour of the day or night, searching every nook and cranny, taking away anything they fancied, and always looking for evidence to justify arresting her or any of her relatives. Her main fears at this time were always for Shanna, but when she realized that amongst the papers they had taken were the details of her sons' education, including where they were studying in Scotland and their addresses, she was afraid for them, particularly as the 'visitors' made a special point of telling her, 'We know where your sons are! Tell them to be careful!'

11

Mehri's Arrest

They came to arrest Mehrangiz at nine o'clock in the morning. It was the 10th of July 1983, exactly one year after the execution of her beloved husband and not long after she had been in hospital for major surgery. Roshanak had gone out to get milk. Mehri was not alone. Her sister and brother-in-law and their daughter were all at home. The bell rang and a voice on the intercom, which was known to all of them, said, 'It's Faríd V here. Some people want to see you.'

When the door was opened to admit him, as a friend they knew and trusted, they found he was accompanied by two Revolutionary Guards. He had given information against her, she was told. The Guards then proceeded to turn the house upside down looking for incriminating evidence.

This was the man to whom she had entrusted Manuchihr's blood-stained clothes, wrapped in a pillowcase hidden inside an old holdall. Mr V had initially stored the holdall in a disused, empty old property of his in Tehran but he became worried that the contents, left inside the holdall, might become smelly, or begin to rot. If the bag were to be left open, then it would be most likely to be invaded by mice, which would damage the clothes beyond repair. What was to be done?

Mr V told Mehri he was trying to send something, unspecified, out of the country. Would she agree that it might be safer to send the clothes out too? Mehri had agreed with him and he had offered to find someone prepared to take them out. His intention was to send them to a relative of his outside Iran, but Mehri does not remember where. Now here he was, seemingly having betrayed her trust, although Mehri refuses to blame him. We do not know what pressure was brought to bear on him, of course, but Mehri would pay a heavy price for it. Apparently, he had found men who would smuggle the items out of the country. They were Afghans, who would buy or 'acquire' cars, load them with goods and slip back across the border into Afghanistan. They were arrested because the Toyota they were driving had no registration number plates and the Civil Police who stopped them suspected that the car itself, and the rugs and valuables inside, were stolen. They were taken to a local police station for routine questioning. Then the police discovered a holdall containing the pillowcase with the bloodstained clothes inside. Instantly, the questioning took a more serious turn.

'You killed someone? Where is the body? Who did you kill?' In vain did the Afghans protest their innocence, indeed their complete ignorance of what was in the holdall. There was quite a commotion as the police became more and more determined to get at the truth. This attracted the attention of the Revolutionary Guards who occupied the top floor of the police station, from where they could monitor the actions of the local police. They took over the interrogation of the two young men. After a severe beating they eventually admitted that the goods in the car were not their property but items they were smuggling for other people. When threatened with more beatings they had stated that the bloodstained clothes had been given to them to take out of the country by Mr V. Faríd V was then arrested. At first he claimed that the clothes were those of his uncle who had been martyred, but under intense interrogation, almost certainly violent, he confessed that Mehrangiz Farzaneh-Moayyad had given them to him.

To this day Mehrangiz refuses to condemn this man for his conduct. She firmly believes that he did the best he could under the circumstances, and still regards him as a friend. Mehri was told she was to be arrested as a spy, accused of sending her husband's clothes out of Iran. Before they took her away, she asked to go to the bathroom. There she removed her wristwatch and ring, engagement presents from Manuchihr, and hid them in the linen basket. She hoped they would not search amongst women's underwear! She asked to say 'goodbye' to her sister, and managed to whisper to her that there was 'something to take care of for me' in the bathroom linen basket. Initially, this jewellery was passed for safe-keeping to a trusted Muslim neighbour, then passed on by her to another person. It was not until Mehri eventually reached freedom that she was able to contact the various people concerned and the jewellery could be returned to her.

Mehri and Mr V were both taken to the same police

station on the outskirts of Tehran where the two hapless smugglers were being held. As they were being driven away, one of the Guards asked her, 'Do you need any medicine?' and stopped at a pharmacy for her. Another whispered, 'I saw your daughter at the neighbour's. She is safe there.' This would seem to indicate that they had been watching the house for some time, or perhaps he was one of those who had already been to search and question them before.

It was Ramadan, when all Muslims are supposed to fast between the hours of sunrise and sunset, but Mehri remembers that at the police station some of the guards were cooking omelettes for themselves. Next day, Mehri was transferred to a Revolutionary Court prison in the north of Tehran. For the first few weeks she was kept in strict solitary confinement and was not allowed any visitors for the first five months. Hers was an infamous prison, allegedly used for political prisoners in the time of the Shah but now accommodating very serious criminals. It was a horrible place, frightening and threatening, where the cells were several floors underground and it was very dark, dank and dingy. The prisoners were always taken upstairs for interrogation sessions, or torture, both mental and physical. Each time she was due to be interrogated she was put into strict solitary confinement for several days beforehand, a 'softening up' technique obviously intended to frighten and demoralize a prisoner.

It was during one of these interrogation sessions that she was violently backhanded across the face, knocking some of her side teeth out. She was accused of spying, trying to send the bloodstained clothes to the United Kingdom or to the United States, 'For President Carter?'

'Not Carter, it's Reagan now!' she replied, perhaps not wisely, but with great spirit. Her purpose, allegedly, was to disgrace the Islamic Republic of Iran. During her first appearance in court she was told that if she became a Muslim she would be freed and all her property would be returned to her. Mehri replied that she preferred to be a human being.

On her first court appearance after being held incommunicado for five months, she was told that she was sentenced to death and would be hanged. She expected it to happen every night after that. Her brother-in-law was in prison at this time and another man, who happened to be in court at the same time as Mehrangiz, told the other Bahá'í prisoners, including her brother-in-law, of her sentence and this was how news of her appearance in court and the sentence became known. One week later she was taken back to court and the death sentence was confirmed.

On one occasion when she was unable to walk she was taken into court on a sort of chair-litter carried by four women prisoners. She was handcuffed to a male officer who walked beside her. The handcuff was very rough and chafed her wrist. When she complained to the man, he was not unsympathetic and loosened it a little, telling her to hold her wrist close to his so that it could not be seen.

All this time Mehri hoped that Shanna did not know about the death sentence. Although Mehri tried to protect her, Shanna found out somehow, as children do, absorbing information as if by a process of osmosis, from a whisper here, an unguarded glance there. Now she had to live with the dreadful fear of losing her mother. Life was very difficult for such a young girl, particularly as she was still trying to cope with the awful shock of losing her beloved father.

Initially, no one knew where Mehri had been taken, or when she would appear in court. Roshanak went to all the likely places she could think of to make enquiries about her mother, visiting all the buildings that she knew were connected to the Revolutionary Court system, but to no avail. When Mehri had been a prisoner for five months, Shanna was told that she could visit her mother, but Mehri was taken to court at six o'clock in the morning, and so on that occasion she was not there when Shanna arrived. When Shanna was finally allowed to see her, Mehri was desperate to hide the fact that some of her teeth had been knocked out and tried very hard not to smile, or even open her mouth and expose the damage. Of course this was almost impossible, and it must have been a very frightening sight for the twelve-year-old.

Eventually Mehri was moved into the main prison building. She remembers going down a long corridor and being shoved through some big gates, or doors, shoved so hard that she almost landed on her face. Prison guards took over from her escort and dragged her along a corridor to a very unpleasant, dark, dirty and smelly area in the basement. She was told this was the quarantine area, 'for dirty ideas'. There was a primus stove here which was kept alight so that the mothers could boil water to feed their babies, but there was very little ventilation and the effect was almost unbearable. When she ventured to ask about fresh air, she was told, 'This is not a hotel, you are here to be punished!'

The accommodation in this place was in bunk beds, in three tiers. Each was equipped with only a thin foam layer instead of a mattress, and these bore many unpleasant traces of previous occupants. There was no bedding. Fleas, lice and bugs were present in abundance. Mehri was kept in this 'quarantine' area for three nights and two days. She was still very unwell both from her illness and the long solitary incarceration, and the unpleasant conditions in which the unfortunate prisoners were expected to survive made everything seem particularly dreadful.

On the third day she was pushed through a small door into a small yard. Here there was a dirty pool in the centre, supposedly for Muslim prayer requirements, and a water tap on a side wall. When she approached this tap to try and get a drink of water, she was prevented from doing so by the other prisoners, who physically assaulted her and yelled, 'It's not your turn!'

In this frightening, hostile environment were serious criminals, each one aggressively defending her own territory. Different sections of this yard were held by different categories of prisoners, and woe-betide any newcomer who did not know the rules.

Eventually, Mehri found a little muddy patch near the pond to which no one else had laid claim. In these squalid conditions, she sat in the mud for three days and three nights as it was too muddy to lie down. She had water to drink, only when she was at last allowed to approach the tap. She was not fed during this time because her name was not on the list for food. She would only be given food when transferred to a cell block. An elderly Bahá'í lady, whose name she has forgotten, came to the rescue and persuaded someone in charge that Mehri very badly needed to be found a bed and to be given food, otherwise she would die there in the yard. An officer found her a space in the same cell as the Bahá'í lady and Mehri's name was entered on the list for food.

Mehri was desperately sick at this time. She managed to remain spiritually strong but physically she was very weak indeed. She was extremely worried about her daughter and the worry had preyed on her mind to such an extent that she was no longer able to remember such things as the names of her two sons. At this time she was in such a low state that she seriously thought she was losing her mind.

Mehri says now that the memory of Manuchihr's bravery made her brave. She was in jail but not afraid to die.

12

Prison

A lot of the experiences of being in prison have run together in Mehri's memory, like one continuous nightmare. She was never able to tell me in a logical sequence how it was and what happened. Recollections surfaced now and then during our many talks together, but often she would find the effort too upsetting and the subject would have to be shelved for another day.

She remembers noise that never stopped and the dirt. The complete discomfort. The smells and the constant crying of the poor babies, incarcerated with their mothers. The cockroaches. The fleas and the lice. The degrading lack of privacy, even for prayer, which was officially forbidden to the Bahá'í prisoners, so that they could only pray silently to themselves. She remembers the initial horror of finding herself in a cell with drug addicts and murderers, who thought a reasonable question to ask her was, 'Who did you kill?' Communication on this level was so far outside her experience of normal life that she found it almost impossible to respond in any meaningful way.

The cell in which she was found a place with the Bahá'í woman had about a dozen three-tier sets of narrow bunks along the walls, and all the available floor space was occupied by another 20 women at least, she estimates.

The drug addicts were the people who made life most difficult for the others, she found. They were a constant menace, fighting and threatening each other continually, and it was often impossible to avoid getting dangerously involved in their warfare. Anybody who had any medication with her had to be on her guard the whole time, for it was always in danger of being stolen by the drug addicts, who were so desperate for a 'fix' that they would take anything and everything. One woman had a particular medication in suppository form with her. The addicts stole them from her and took them like everything else. At least it gave them all something to smile about, even a little joking speculation about the probable effects on the human constitution, but it did not seem to do the particular addict any harm.

These were people who seemed to have sunk as low as it is possible for a human being to sink and yet, sometimes, she found they were still capable of the odd kindness to a fellow prisoner.

Occasionally there were acts of kindness from the jailors. One day, a warder had escorted her to the washroom for a shower. On leaving, the woman hissed at her, 'Forget your comb. Leave it behind.'

Startled, but obedient, Mehri did so, albeit reluctantly, as it was the only comb she had.

Returned to the cell, the woman pushed her in and berated her with, 'You left your comb? What a nuisance you are. I will see about it later.'

She left, but returned shortly and escorted Mehri back to the washroom. Shoving her over the threshold without ceremony the woman said, 'Now get your comb and hurry up. I'll come back for you soon.'

Mehri had a wonderful surprise. Waiting there for her was another prisoner. It was her dear cousin. Mehri did not know that her cousin had been sent to prison and had been asking everyone she met if they knew Mehrangiz and where she was. Now her cousin had managed to make contact, it was a lifeline for both of them. The cousin's husband had also been sent to prison at the same time, although he was in a different establishment for male prisoners and she had almost no contact with him. He was to die in prison, of a heart attack, no doubt brought on by the stress and uncertainty of their situation, and the knowledge that his dear wife was also a prisoner. Neither of them was ever charged with any offence other than that of being members of the Bahá'í Faith.

Mehrangiz and her cousin were overjoyed to see each other, as one might imagine, despite the horrible circumstances. It was this cousin that Mehri had telephoned about her dream when Manuchihr was killed. On this occasion they were allowed only a little time together before Mehri was taken back to her cell, but when she confided that her illness had affected her memory to the extent that she could not remember the names of her children, her cousin was able to give her the information and to reassure her that such a thing was probably due to shock and would be only temporary.

The meeting was a great boost for Mehri, who no longer felt quite so alone. Indeed, it was almost as if she had been reunited with her 'forgotten' children. Mehri had no idea how the warder knew that she was related to another prisoner. She found out years later that her cousin knew of Mehri's arrest and imprisonment long before she was herself arrested. Once in the prison system, she asked everyone where her cousin Mehri was, until at last she had found a young Muslim woman who had shared a cell with her.

Eventually Mehrangiz was able to persuade someone in authority to allow her cousin to be moved into the already overcrowded cell, where there were other Bahá'í prisoners. This immediately improved Mehri's conditions, at least in a spiritual sense. Her cousin had been kept in prison for almost one year when her husband died. His body, which bore no marks of torture, although he had been badly beaten during interrogation, was released to his family for burial, and his wife was told she would be allowed to leave the prison for the funeral. When she queried this she was told that it had only ever been their intention to keep her a prisoner for one year anyway, so as soon as the year was up she would be free. And indeed she was freed, having lost her husband and spent a year of her life in the most atrocious conditions imaginable, without the comfort of having any contact with him.

While in prison all the Bahá'í women tried to remain positive for each other, doing what little they could to support each other and to alleviate the situation for all of them. It was very comforting for Mehri to have this help from a member of her own family, someone who was able to remind her of the names of the boys, because this was something she had found very frightening and desperately worrying. She thought such details should be unforgettable to a mother under any circumstances and her cousin's calm assurances helped her immeasurably. No doubt her cousin found the same sort of comfort in contact with Mehri, who could understand and empathize completely with all her worries for her husband and her own children.

The many sessions of interrogation that Mehri had to endure were always difficult. When one man lashed out with his fist, hitting her in the face and knocking out some teeth, her main reaction was amazement that anyone could do such a thing. In all her life no one had ever struck her in anger. Through the blood and the tears that flowed automatically, she struggled to remain calm, even when she was told that it was their intention to exterminate all the Bahá'ís in Iran, to 'cleanse the world of all Bahá'ís', to which she responded fearlessly.

'When you killed my husband, his nephew who lives in Canada arranged a memorial service for him. Five hundred people attended, and it was shown on television to thousands of people. Much good publicity for us. Every week there is a half hour programme on their television station, people are asking lots of questions and they are becoming Bahá'ís. Every Bahá'í has friends and relatives who are spreading the word. So I ask God to give the Ayatollah (Khomeini) long life so that he can continue his work of spreading the Bahá'í Faith for us!'

Late one night Mehri was taken from the cell. She

thought that she was to be executed or interrogated, and concentrated all her mental strength on preparing herself spiritually, repeating and repeating to herself the name of God. For many weeks now she had expected this every night. This time, she was escorted to another part of the prison. Here she was put into a cell and made to listen to the screams of a young girl coming from an adjacent cell.

'Listen to your daughter!' the guards jeered at her.

The sounds were horrendous and heart rending, and seemed to go on forever. Mehri was close to collapse when the man who had taken her there whispered, in an attempt to comfort her, 'It is not YOUR daughter.'

But Mehri could find no comfort in that. Indeed what sort of a human being would be able to find comfort in the fact that it was someone else's child?

'If not my daughter, she is someone's daughter,' she replied.

Mehri does not know how long she was forced to stay there or how long this torture lasted, but eventually she was returned to the cell, where her cellmates had spent the time quietly praying for her safe return. They were very glad that she was unharmed, but horrified when she told them what she had been forced to listen to. Now she was tormented by new fears for Shanna's safety.

Shanna was having a very difficult time while Mehri was in prison. She was naturally consumed by grief for her father and terrified at the prospect of losing her mother, because somehow she knew of Mehri's death sentence, although no one had told her. She was crying every day, at home and at school, where she confided in a sympathetic school friend who she thought understood her situation. This girl, no doubt horrified and thinking the adults would be able to help Shanna, reported to the teachers that Roshanak had told her that her father had been executed and her mother was in prison, sentenced to death. The headmistress asked her guardian to attend a meeting, at which the head and all the teachers were present.

'Roshanak', the headmistress said, 'has told the children something very dreadful, and the children came to me.'

Shanna was summoned to the meeting. The headmistress was very nice to her.

'If your father and mother are very bad people,' she said, 'you should not be ashamed. Do not worry. Do not cry for them. It is not your fault. We will care for you and help you to become a good Muslim.'

Shanna stood up to her bravely. 'I only cry because I miss my parents very much, but I am not ashamed. I love them and I am very proud of them.'

The head became very cross and struck her, telling her to get out.

So Shanna left that school too.

It is possible that Mehri's weakened state protected her from physical torture during this time, for the officials would not have wanted her to die under torture, as she might well have done, because they wanted her strong enough to hang. Ironically, it was the official insistence on a prisoner being able to stand up unaided while the sentence of hanging was carried out that was eventually to provide Mehri with the opportunity to escape from both the prison system and Iran. Because she was so weakened by the blood loss before her operation and the trauma of the operation itself and, before that, the shock of her husband's death, and because she had never had any chance to recuperate from any of that, it is incredible that she survived at all. What she really needed was a large blood transfusion, vitamin injections, good food, fresh air, plenty of rest and nothing to worry about. Instead she was kept in prison like a common criminal and treated as badly, if not worse, than many of them. She had been in prison for many months now, her condition was steadily worsening, her weight being perhaps around five and a half stones (about 80 lb/35 kg) at the most at this time, and she was so weak that it was difficult to stand or walk without assistance. She was suffering badly from arthritis and was eating very little, mainly due to the fact that as her teeth had been knocked out, it was too painful to eat the dull, dry, unappetizing prison food.

In the prison system, executions were carried out either at dawn or very late at night. From the time she was given the death sentence. Mehri lived with the knowledge, indeed the expectation, that each day would be her last. She tried always to prepare herself according to a ḥadíth (tradition) attributed to the Imám 'Alí, the son-in-law of the Prophet Muhammad: 'Strive for this life as though thou wouldst live eternally, and strive for the next as though thou wouldst die tomorrow.'

Consequently, when she was called out very early one morning, she believed the time had come. Instead, almost unbelievably, she was told she was to go to a hospital and seek treatment. She was instructed to report back to the prison three days later. Whoever thought that three days was going to be sufficient time to bring her back to a reasonable state of health clearly had no understanding of what her situation was, but that was exactly what she was told. When she dutifully returned to the prison to be readmitted, at the time she had been instructed to report, she was turned away with a casual comment to the effect that as she was supported by two friends and was not standing alone, she was clearly still unfit for their purposes. She was to go away and seek further treatment, and this time they would come for her when it was thought that she had recovered sufficiently.

Instead of staying with her relatives in Tehran, she decided to go back to live in Qazvin. The house that Manuchihr had put into the names of their sons had been confiscated when he was arrested but the official at the court who had been so grateful to her brother, Dr Ṣamadání, for saving his mother's life, had told her that she would be able to have two rooms there if she wanted to live in them. She decided she would go and see him and ask him if the offer was still open. She did so, and it was. He gave her the two rooms by the simple expedient of relocating the tenants who had been moved into Mehri's family home. Among them were some hardliners who had been housed upstairs, the officer telling Mehri that she would get on better with the new tenants he was installing, as indeed she did, because they were to become trusted friends.

13

The Escape . . . from Qazvin

The chance to escape came unexpectedly one day, as such things tend to.

Soheil R had come to give Mehri her usual injection. Soheil was a young would-be medical student who was having to train 'on the job' as a doctor, which was the only way open to him since he had been refused university entrance on the grounds of his religion. He told her that he would not be able to come anymore because he had an opportunity to get out and he was going to take it. It might be the only chance he would ever have to escape to a country where he would be able to study and qualify as a doctor. He was leaving the very next day.

Mehri thought of Roshanak. Whatever she might want to do with her life would be impossible if they stayed. Denied an education, the girl had little or no future. If they stayed, Mehri would inevitably be taken back to prison, and soon Shanna would have no mother, for Mehri had no hope that the death sentence would not be carried out. Almost two years had elapsed since she had been turned away from the prison to seek further treatment so that she would become strong enough to be hanged and she knew that at any time they would be looking for her. She also knew that it had been their intention to arrest her daughter at the same time she was arrested and that it was only by chance that Shanna had been out on an errand to buy milk at the time. On her return she was warned by a friendly Muslim neighbour not to go home because the house was surrounded by guards. So, simply because of her beliefs and those of her parents, Shanna also was in great danger.

Mehri knew she was very far from well and that the rigours of the journey the young man was contemplating would be very difficult for her – might even kill her – but at the same time, here was a possible chance for both her and her daughter. She had always known that some people had escaped but had never known anyone involved in the process or how to go about finding such people. Mehri knew she could not turn away from this God-given opportunity, which might never be repeated. She begged to be included in the party with her young daughter.

Getting out of Iran was a complex and highly dangerous undertaking. Those involved in making the arrangements were not, in the main, motivated by altruism. They smuggled contraband for the Mujahaddin and people when the price was right. It was rumoured that there had been cases of people trying to escape who had simply been taken into the desert and murdered for their valuables. Or they had been handed over to the authorities. Or robbed and abandoned, in the mountains or the desert, to die of exposure. Sometimes of course there were happy results, when someone would telephone, after long weeks or months of silence, to announce that they were safe and well and out of the country. Mehri had heard rumours of such calls. She knew that she wanted just such a chance. She would pray, and put her trust in God and her life in the hands of strangers. For what alternative was there, except to stay and do nothing, which would eventually leave her daughter to face a motherless future?

In view of Mehri's fragile state of health, the young man was initially reluctant to include them in the party, but eventually he was persuaded that it was a very logical thing for her to do. In fact, he agreed that there really was no choice for her in the matter and went to see if he could make the necessary arrangements with the smugglers, leaving Mehri to find a way to raise the substantial funds required to finance the venture. Later that evening Soheil returned to the house and told Mehri that both she and Shanna could go but they were setting out at ten o'clock the next morning and she would need to have the money with her at that time.

Mehri already knew that they would not be able to carry any luggage with them. They could not afford to risk any appearance of starting out on a long journey, so they would be able to take only what they could carry in their hands or on their persons. They would have to be prepared to face a journey of perhaps nine or ten days. It would probably be very uncomfortable. It would certainly be exhausting. There could be no doubt at all that it would also be very dangerous, both for the fugitives, and for their escorts. Perhaps fortunately, at this stage she had very little idea of what her leaving would actually entail.

The financial side was taken care of when an acquaintance offered to buy everything in the house from her and paid a very generous price of 50,000 túmáns, which was approximately £2,500. Living upstairs were new lodgers, friendly, moderate Muslims who so far had not paid any rent to anyone. When they heard of her plans, they immediately produced another 50,000 túmáns in lieu of rent, because they wanted to help her.

Mehri confided her plans to another trusted neighbour, a Muslim woman who was very alarmed and tried to persuade her not to go, telling her scary stories she had heard of the smugglers who were all thieves and vagabonds apparently, although she had never had any dealings with them, of course. This woman and her husband had been completely opposed to the Bahá'ís – they had been part of the Islamic regime in fact – until their son was executed for joining a leftist opposition group, and they began to view the Revolutionary Government in a very different light. The neighbour had even told Mehri at one point that she would become a Bahá'í if she could, but feared it was just too dangerous for her.

When the neighbour realized that Mehri was not to be dissuaded, her help took a more practical turn and she presented the travellers with large bags of dates and pistachio nuts, halva and figs, which they would eventually be very glad of, for the time would come when they would rely on them as their only sustenance. When Mehri and Shanna were safely in the UK, this woman would send parcels of warm clothing for Shanna. All these people were true friends.

They left Qazvin the very next day and travelled to Tehran on a public bus, a journey that took nearly four hours. There were seven Bahá'ís in all, but they did not travel together, having been instructed that it was safer if they all ignored each other on this first stage of the journey. Mehri and Shanna were wearing correct Islamic dress, wide long trousers and big overcoats, and each wore a headscarf that completely covered her hair. In Tehran they met up with the smugglers who gave them further instructions. They were to go by bus to A, a journey of another 11 or 12 hours. This was not over good roads and they were badly jolted for most of the journey. Eventually they reached their destination and met two of the smugglers, who were Afghanis, as Mehri described them, 'educated, normal, nice young men', wearing western dress. Here transport was provided in the form of some sort of pick-up van, probably a Ford Transit, to B, a small village on the edge of the desert, where villagers provided basic accommodation and provisions for them all. Outside B, they walked into the desert and stopped to rest, waiting for transport the smugglers had described as 'the Phoenix'. Since no such bird exists, it was probably not so surprising that it failed to materialize. Eventually, word came that the Russians had closed the road on the Afghanistan side where it was supposed to be coming from. It was decided that in this area, the noise of the engine would give them away, and it was probably too dangerous to use it. They would have to walk to another rendezvous to pick up their transport.

There followed a gruelling trek through the desert

terrain for another hour or two. Mehri was in poor shape and almost had to be carried by some of the others. When they reached the rendezvous, there was still no sign of the elusive 'Phoenix'. Eventually, to the consternation of all the escapees, seven camels, which were already fully loaded, arrived to convey them on the next stage of this journey. This was not how they had expected to travel, but there appeared to be no alternative available, so they would just have to accept it.

For the fugitives, the trek across the desert was by far the most taxing part of their long journey. City dwellers for the most part, they found the alien territory hostile and threatening, and they were ill-equipped to cope with the rigours of travelling by camel. Mehri had never even seen a camel before, except in pictures, and any idea of an animal with some sort of seat for its rider was soon dispelled. The seven animals that made up the caravan were so heavily laden with the goods they were trafficking to the Mujahaddin in Afghanistan who were fighting a guerilla war with the Russians who had invaded that country in 1979, that there was no room for anything resembling a saddle. This was not the nice ride in the desert as offered to tourists by camel drivers in such places as Egypt, for example. The Arabian camel has only one hump, unlike the Bactrian camel which has two and the passenger sits between them. The Arabian camel offers no support for the back, only a rope to hold onto, and Shanna clutched this rope so tightly that a little gold ring on her finger was broken into several pieces. The lurching, angular gait of these 'ships of the desert' resulted in a strange rocking motion to which it was difficult for the novices to accustom themselves. The camels were so laden that the passengers had to balance themselves precariously on top of all the boxes and bundles, 'like afterthoughts', says Mehri, with their legs sticking out at very uncomfortable angles or with knees bent awkwardly. Any position quickly became extremely painful, so much so that when they halted for a brief rest, none of them were able to stand unaided. Mehri and some of the others had to be lifted down and placed on the sand to wait until the pain subsided and the circulation returned to their legs. The arthritis that had started to trouble her in prison made her condition worse. All her fellow travellers, even the young men, were in nearly as bad a shape as she was. During these brief rest periods their guides showed them how to scrape little hollows in the sand to lie in, and how to cover themselves with sand to keep warm, because nighttime in the desert can be very cold indeed. This helped a little but the sand penetrated everything, which added greatly to their overall discomfort. The thick black clothes that Mehri and Shanna were dressed in did not help either, particularly in the heat of the day. Black absorbs heat, and the wearer can find it stifling and extremely uncomfortable. In countries where women are accorded a lower status than men, the men usually get to wear bright dazzling white, which reflects the heat and keeps the wearer much cooler, whilst the women are shrouded in heat-absorbing black, often in heavy fabrics that will not move even in a breeze. There was also the need to watch out for snakes and scorpions in the desert, which did not add to their comfort at all, and even less to their peace of mind.

One extremely dark night when they were travelling by camel, the guides were very jumpy because they had to cross a road on the border with Afghanistan that was heavily patrolled by the Russians. Instructions to the fugitives were clear and emphatic – NO NOISE UNDER ANY CIRCUMSTANCES – for sound travels at night. Even the occasional snort from a camel sounded alarmingly loud. They had crossed the road safely when Mehri heard a cry and became aware that Shanna's camel was missing. In a panic she called out to the young men who came running back and angrily told her to be quiet. She believes now that they probably knew that the other camel would catch up with its fellows at some point; she also realizes that whilst the loss of one young girl might mean very little to them, they would not have been prepared to abandon a camel and all its precious cargo. However, in response to her whispered pleas one of them went back along the trail and eventually, after what seemed like hours, he appeared, leading the missing animal with Shanna still perched on top. What had happened was that as soon as the beast got onto the hard road, it had decided to sit down for a rest, letting the others go on without it. Nothing that Shanna could do had made any difference to the stubborn beast. It simply stayed where it was until its owner appeared. Now they can laugh about it, but it must have been extremely frightening when it happened.

From her home in Australia Roshanak described her experience.

The incident with the camel was very scary. We had to cross a road which was heavily guarded. Mine was the last camel and mum's was somewhere ahead. They had told us not to make a sound, and if anyone fell behind, well, bad luck! When my camel sat down in the middle of the road the first thing I did was scream for mum, which I think helped because the guide came back for me. It was pitch black and very, very scary. To this day I do not like camels! I respect them of course, as one should, but I cannot stand them.

Mehri recalls seeing skeletons of camels in this border area but nowhere else. In all probability they had been killed in skirmishes across the border, so the danger they were in was very real.

After the incident with Shanna's camel, the fugitives continued on their wearisome journey. They were all exhausted, distressingly dirty and dusty. They were extremely hungry and very thirsty. Adding to their miserable condition was the constant fear of discovery, which went with them like a shadow, so that even in the vastness of the desert they were unable to relax, the tension adding to their physical discomfort.

Given the state of her health before starting out on this venture, it was no surprise that Mehri was soon obviously very ill, so ill that even the guides noticed, although she made no complaint. One of them became so concerned about her that he insisted on giving her water from his own goatskin bag. Years later, she shudders at the memory.

'I knew it was full of "spiders"', she said, groping for an acceptable English translation of 'water-borne organisms and bacteria' and failing to find one. Ever pragmatic, she calculated that she would probably die of thirst long before the microbes in the bag could harm her, so, putting her trust in God, she drank, gratefully, and survived to tell the tale.

14

The Escape . . . to Lahore

In a decent, settled society, where life might be expected to follow predictable patterns, Mehrangiz and Manuchihr would have lived out their lives as honourable, upright, respected citizens. Mehri's life would have been that of any woman married to a successful man, with an ordered, tranquil home, well-educated children and a secure future. She would have continued to wear nice clothes, drive her own car, and keep herself beautifully groomed, enjoying the increased prosperity that comes from hard work and a sensible lifestyle. She would have continued giving stylish dinner parties for family and friends, and hosting large gatherings for her Bahá'í community, in a house where the dining room could comfortably seat two dozen people or more, and a chef would be employed for these special occasions. This had been her life. Now her husband was dead and here she was, a fleeing fugitive, in fear for her life and the life of her precious daughter.

At a nomadic Bedouin camp where the fugitives gratefully accepted food and shelter, Mehri was amazed to see a young child, a boy about three or four years old, who was still breast feeding from his mother. It was not only the fact that he was still breast feeding that amazed her, however. Leaning nonchalantly against his mother whilst he satisfied himself, the child held a lighted cigarette in his hand. As soon as he dropped the nipple, he carried on smoking, glaring suspiciously at Mehri when he noticed her watching him. This shocking image made a lasting impression on Mehrangiz. At the time, it was explained to her, it was thought that tobacco was being made easily available to these relatively unsophisticated people in an attempt to get them addicted and therefore easily controlled and manipulated. The truth of the matter is not for debate here; Mehri reports only what she saw for herself and what she was told as explanation.

This Bedouin encampment was a strange place in the middle of the desert. There was no permanent water supply and the huts were very basic mud ones, with a roof and curtained walls. These hospitable tribal people herded goats and sheep. They were very kind and helpful to the exhausted travellers, and fed them plenty of meat and milk. Whatever they had for themselves was shared with their guests. No doubt they were rewarded for their efforts but Mehri remembers particularly their kindness and consideration for their guests.

Leaving the Bedouin camp after a good rest, the camel ride continued. At some point they had crossed the border into Afghanistan and travelled along the border towards C where they left the camel train behind, with very little reluctance, it must be said. From there they eventually changed to proper motorized transport, but this was not the blessing it seemed to be at first, for it was an open back truck, full of smuggled goods and this time two armed gunmen were lying full length on top of the cargo, on guard. The goods were covered by a thick layer of some sort of foam material in big rolls. The fugitives had to sit where they could between the gunmen and on top of the goods. Mehri ended up in a corner where the foam was thickest. She started to sink right into it. The truck was jolting up and down sand dunes, throwing the passengers about violently. Mehri's knees were right up to her chin. She was in danger of suffocating and became completely stuck, but the driver refused to stop. It was just too dangerous. When the driver thought it safe he stopped and the men pulled her out. This nightmare journey in the truck lasted for a whole day. Eventually they arrived at another place on the border between Afghanistan and Pakistan, a Mujahaddin camp at D. Here they spent a few hours resting and recovering.

They were given Afghan clothes to wear, which for the women was not a pleasant change. The clothes were in a very thick cloth which completely covered them, with only a mesh in front of their eyes so that, theoretically, they could see but not be seen. Actually it was possible to see very little. The clothes were very dirty and had obviously had lots of previous occupants. For the fastidious Mehri this was a trial almost on a par with her experiences in prison, but she was determined that they were going to escape and each unpleasantness was only getting them closer to their goal. They were told that as females they were to keep silent at all times in public, for the Taliban were active in the area and were very actively suppressing whatever was deemed to be unseemly conduct by women. Since this could vary considerably, no one was quite sure what passed as acceptable, at least in the eyes of the radical Taliban.

The next stage of the journey was by public transport across the border and into Pakistan to E. This bus journey was described by Mehri as horrific and was an epic in itself. She remembers the bus as dangerously overcrowded, incredibly smelly and very, very dirty. Everybody was packed in so tightly that when it stopped, passengers from the back who wanted to get off would have to resort to literally walking on top of the other passengers. People stood on Mehri's head, and on Shanna's, more than once. The overpowering smell was so awful that it was hard to breathe most of the time, for the bus carried not only passengers but included their livestock, mainly chickens, that many of the passengers were taking with them.

Eventually, after what seemed like many hours, the bus arrived at F and they were safely in Pakistan. Here the fugitives were met by a local Bahá'í man with whom the smugglers must have been in touch. He took them all to a small local hotel. The man had provided Pakistani clothes for them all, so the Afghan ones could be handed back to the smugglers. The travellers parted from their guides with real joy, gratitude and affection, for they had shared so much in the previous nine days that they felt great bonds of kinship and friendship with these young men, who had kept all their promises at considerable risk to themselves.

The Pakistani clothes were so different that Mehri was shocked at first. The fabrics were very light and thin compared to those they had been forced to wear, and very colourful. The shalwar kameez, loose shirts and light trousers, seemed to be the normal wear. A long scarf, like a sash, had to be worn over one shoulder. Apparently, that was important because it indicated a 'decent' woman. One was not considered 'respectable' without it. For the Indian women who chose to wear the sari, a bare midriff was deemed to be perfectly acceptable, but only if the sash was worn at the same time. Mehri was scandalized!

At the hotel, other local Bahá'ís came to meet them. Then a representative of the National Spiritual Assembly of Pakistan came. He would decide where to send them next. Mehri and Shanna stayed there about three days, to give Mehri time to rest. After that they were sent on to Lahore where they were received by the chairman of the National Assembly. He took Mehri to a doctor for treatment, which she badly needed by this time, although the relief of being safe had given her a tremendous psychological boost. With the resilience of the young, Shanna was recovering quickly from the strenuous trek and was just so happy to be safely out of Iran.

The doctor's surgery was a revelation to Mehrangiz. Diplomas in medicine from Harvard and from the United Kingdom, as well as those from Pakistan, decorated the walls. Proper, qualified treatment at last. Now Mehri knew her survival was assured. They found accommodation in a small quiet guest house. This was a peaceful place, but any arrivals at night would panic Shanna and she had to run and check that their door was locked. The terrible fear of intruders in the night, which was entirely reasonable given her experiences, would stay with her for many years to come.

On their first day in Lahore they were taken to an office of the United Nations to register as refugees and be issued with identity cards. Pakistani authorities were likely to arrest anyone without ID, they were told. The UN official listened to Mehri's story and recognized her condition, and the cards were issued immediately. Mehri contacted Farshid and Fardin from Lahore to tell them that they were safe. Naturally her sons were overjoyed and were impatient for them to travel to the UK as soon as it would be possible. Having been granted full refugee status, Mehri was told that she could choose where she would like to go and had opted for the UK as her sons were there. Now they just had to wait until all the documentation was completed and she was pronounced fit to travel. The rest of their stay in Lahore was peaceful. A Muslim country, there was no animosity towards them as Bahá'ís. If anyone asked why they had come to Pakistan, Mehri would reply, 'Because we are Bahá'ís,' and the response would always be calm, welcoming and reassuring.

Mehri was still quite ill while they were in Lahore. Once she fell in the street, and a man called out urgently to Shanna, 'Come help your mother, she is going to die in the street!' but Mehri knew she would not die just yet. As soon as she was well enough she and Shanna left for Scotland.

In 1988, about two years after she arrived in the United

Kingdom, the Universal House of Justice, the supreme governing body of the Bahá'ís, asked Mehrangiz to go to Geneva for three days to consult with the committee concerned with human rights. She travelled alone and was met in Geneva by two Bahá'ís who escorted her to a hotel and then to the committee meetings on each day. There were three days of very formal interviews, very intensive, but at no time did Mehri feel under any pressure. These people wanted to know the truth and were prepared to listen to her. A representative of the United Nations Committee for Human Rights was present, and also there were several other people whose names and functions she does not recall. All the proceedings were recorded.

She received a card dated 27 April 1988 (translated from Farsi):

> Greatly appreciate your acceptance of our invitation to come and share with us your experiences, and to speak to the Representative from the Committee for Human Rights, and for telling them of your treatment in Iran and of the treatment of the other Bahá'ís in Iran. When the Delegate has reported back, a copy of the report will be sent to you in due course.

Mehri did receive a copy of the report, and a covering letter from the UN, but unfortunately it went out of her possession and was 'lost' to her family. This little card is all she has left to remind her of that visit.

It is amazing that Mehri was able to survive this

experience and this journey, but in many ways she has suffered, and continues to suffer, the consequences of the ill-treatment she received in Iran. Consequences both physical and mental have sapped her strength, but never her resilience.

15

Roshanak's Story

As a very young girl, Roshanak was more directly involved with the horrendous events that befell her family than either of her brothers, who were forced by circumstances into the role of helpless bystanders, unable to help or support the family except from a great distance. Shanna was ten years old when the aunt she loved very much, Mrs Bahíyyih Nádirí, was abducted. They had enjoyed a family party the evening before to say 'goodbye' to Fardin, the younger of her two brothers who was returning to the UK after a brief visit. Mrs Nádirí left the house to go to a meeting, then suddenly she was gone and would never be seen again. How frightening in itself that one event must have been for a child but for Shanna it was just the start of years of terror.

In response to my questions she says, in her own words:

> I do not remember how many schools I was kicked out of because of my Faith and my parents but I remember joking that as every two or three months I was in need of a new school, I was soon going to run out of options. As for difficulties, yes, they were all horrible in such a way that even now I dislike schools and have no good memories of my school years.

I remember being alone, usually because I was told that if people found out who I was and about my situation, I would not be allowed to go to school, yet again. Also that I could be made a ward of the state, which meant that I would be sent to an orphanage.

At religious study classes they would 'bad mouth' and insult the Bahá'ís, the Báb, Bahá'u'lláh and 'Abdu'l-Bahá (the son of Bahá'u'lláh). It was very hard to keep quiet at such times and I did not always manage it. I would stand up to answer back and would say what I had to say, but I would be shaking so much, not with fear but out of anger and rage at their ignorance. How could they judge me, my family and my Faith without reading even one single line from one of our books? I cannot recall how many times I was told to 'shut up', or told to get out of the classroom by the teacher, who would throw books or pens or anything that came to hand at me. I would sit alone and cry, then I would be called to the principal's office. At first they would talk kindly to me and tell me not to be ashamed of my family – I could choose to be different. When I would tell them that I was proud of my family they would give me my marching orders!

One of my worst memories was when I had my first birthday after dad was killed. Mum tried to make it a happy time for me and gave a party for me. I invited three or four people from my class who I thought would be nice. The next day one of them came back to the house and asked for the return of the gift she had given me.

'Because I knew you were a Bahá'í but I didn't know your father was killed. My mother and father don't want anyone to know I know you, or was ever at your house!'

I gave her back the present.

I cannot recall how many times I have had to defend my Faith and my family, but somehow I always managed to. And I would always go and ask the teachers for a day off for the Bahá'í holy days. Once I told some of my classmates that as Bahá'ís we have to investigate the truth individually, not just accept it because our parents followed that religion. I did not have to be a Bahá'í if, after studying other religions I decided not to, so during the class one of my friends asked the teacher if, as Muslims, they could read about other religions. The teacher said yes, there was no problem with that, but when the girl asked if she would be able to change and embrace another religion, that was when the teacher said she should be killed for doing that, 'your blood should be spilt', was how she put it. I then stood up and said that the good thing about the Bahá'í Faith is that we do have a free choice! The response from the teacher was to tell me to shut up and sit down, no one had asked for my opinion!

I remember the day dad was taken. Mum was unwell and I picked up the phone. Some man said, 'I am so-and-so calling from Qazvin and we have (arrested) your father.' I cried out to mum that they had my dad, then mum took the phone and spoke to the guy.

At that time it felt as if part of my heart was cut off. During all the time he was imprisoned, and later, my mum kept her head high and carried on with such strength and dignity, never showing fear, or hurt, or anger. When I said something such as, 'I wish things were different,' she would say, 'No, this is what is meant to be. This is God's wish, so as Bahá'ís we accept it.'

I know how hard it was for her. I saw how much she suffered in silence, but what could I do?

I remember when we went to visit dad, she would tell me, 'No matter how sad or sick you are, you are never to let dad know how hard life is for us, as this may affect him badly. The decisions that he has to make are his, between him and God. There must be no external influences. Also he should be happy.'

So as a result, when we went to the prison, even if I was feeling ill, I would try and be happy and say everything was well with us. Mum did just the same too.

During one visit, it was Ramadan, during the hot Iranian summer, I got very sick due to dehydration and felt really weak and started vomiting. One of the guards brought me some water to drink, even though to be seen to eat or drink during the fasting month could get one severely punished, even children.

When dad was killed we heard from a phone call, but not from the prison, 'they' never told us. Mum went to Qazvin with some family or friends, I am not sure. Somehow I tried not to believe what had happened. I saw people coming and my cousin would tell them something. Later on I found out that she would tell them, 'Shana is not certain what has happened, so take off your black coats and don't ask, or tell her, anything until her mum comes back.'

When mum eventually came back, her cousin's husband came in first so I ran and asked him, 'Did you see dad? How was he?'

He said, 'His spirit is happy and well.'

I remember screaming and running out of the room in disbelief.

I asked mum, 'Why didn't you take me with you? And when you called before and I asked you about him you said, "Yes, I saw him and he's sent a letter for you and your brothers."'

She said, 'I didn't take you because I want you always to remember your dad when he was alive, not his dead face. Also, yes, I did see the body, and the letter I mentioned is his will.'

On the morning that mum was taken from our home I had gone to the bakery to get some bread. Mum thinks now that I had gone for milk, but I remember it was bread. I came back and saw from a distance that the Revolutionary Guards were at the house. I did hide at a neighbour's house for a long time. Later on I heard my cousin's voice calling me but at the same time signalling me to stay away. When I went home much later, mum was gone! I did not see or hear from her for the next five months. During this time I went to all the court houses, jails and any other places where we thought she might be. To no avail.

During this time I went from one home to another.

Everywhere I went, someone was taken to prison and every single time I was interrogated, with guns pointed at my face and threats.

They said, 'Give us information about other Bahá'ís and we will let your mother go.'

I never believed them and tried to stand up to them.

The first time I visited mum was bliss. I could not believe she was alive. Knowing that my mother who loved me so much was alive helped me to feel not so lonely and alone in the world. No one could really understand me. I was 12 years old. No father or mother. People all had their own problems and dealing with me was an extra effort no one needed, so seeing mum was like getting my life back. Although I did tell her to be strong like dad, she asked, 'Do you know what that means and what could happen?' and I said, 'Yes.'

I did not tell her about my loneliness, the endless nights crying in the dark, no one knowing how I felt. The feelings of despair, and the fear of being taken away to an orphanage.

I cannot thank God enough for giving her back to me. I don't know how I coped with being alone, not knowing where I would end up. I must have had help from above, after all, I have many family and friends there, and I believe they were looking out for me!

I did not care at all about our materialistic things being taken from us, but every time something of sentimental value was taken, such as the bit of earth from dad's grave, it was a huge blow to me. When someone was killed or imprisoned a little piece of me died too.

When I realized that we could escape I was sad to leave our family and friends behind. I felt guilty and worried about what would happen to dad's grave. But the thought of losing mum if we stayed was so frightening that it outweighed any other feelings. Also the prospect of seeing my beloved brothers was unimaginably wonderful.

The camel incident was very scary but lots of other things on that trek distracted me. The journey was very difficult but it was a means to the freedom I craved, so it had to be. At least we escaped. So many others couldn't.

As for the after effects, well I do not think I have done too badly. I am a lot more cautious of people than one should be. It takes me a long time to trust people. I still have nightmares, which must go back to my childhood. My family is everything to me. I do feel free, but at the same time not really. It is as if I can't really believe it is true. I have no feelings for Iran, except that it is the birthplace of the Faith and it is where dad is. If it were not for those two reasons I would never think about it. Scotland to me is home. That is where for the first time I saw people truly liking me for me, not my religion. The first place that I felt truly safe and started to trust people. Then Australia became my second home.

I can still see the results of what happened to me and my family in my thoughts, beliefs, attitudes and behaviour; the way I double and triple check locks on the doors; the way I worry about my mum, my kids, my brothers and their kids, and about losing them.

It makes me sad when I see people caring about jobs, titles and status; the size of their houses or the clothes they wear. People are dying, giving their lives for their beliefs. Why care about silly things? This angers me. Don't take me wrong, I like nice things as much as the next person, but sometimes the material-ism of people puzzles me. I just have to think that it is their life, not mine.

I am very lucky to have gone through what I have. I have learnt a lot and am more than proud of my mum and dad. I saw so many wonderful people, so many sacrifices that it makes me feel humble and privileged to have met these wonderful people. Most important of all I am grateful for being a Bahá'í and having had mum and dad's guidance. I hope I could be as good a parent to my kids as they were to me.

Shanna M.

16

Epilogue
Where are They Now?

Mehrangiz Farzaneh-Moayyad lives quietly in Scotland, in the city where her two sons were sent to continue their education. It was always intended that they would return to Iran but the revolution in 1979 made that impossible. When the UN granted Mehri refugee status in 1985, she was allowed to choose where she would like to go and opted for Scotland because both her sons were living there. Her experiences have left her health permanently impaired but her spirit is indomitable. Whenever the opportunity occurs she is willing to talk about her life, either to individuals or to the media, giving interviews to the press or to the radio with the same unassuming gentleness that characterizes her general attitude to life.

Farshid, the eldest son, is married to Rose, and they have one daughter. They live about 20 miles from his mother and they visit her as often as possible, although his work frequently takes him abroad for long periods.

Speaking of his experiences, especially finding himself fatherless in such appalling circumstances, he says, 'I was out of step with my contemporaries – all their interests and topics of conversation seemed so trivial and point-less, compared to what was going on in my life.'

He felt 'closed off' from his fellow students and found it impossible to burden anyone else with his concerns. He would think of his family and what was happening to them and feel absolutely helpless to do anything. When his father was killed, he and Fardin had packed their bags and were prepared to return to Iran, desperate to be with their mother and sister. They understood the reasons that Mehri gave them for not wanting them to return but it was very hard to respect her wishes at that time. Even now he still finds it difficult to talk of trivialities.

The younger son, Fardin, also married in Scotland and has two sons. He is divorced from his first wife and now lives in the USA. He has remarried and sees his sons whenever he can. They still live in Scotland, near their grandmother.

The events in Iran meant great hardship for the two boys living in Scotland, because they no longer had any financial support and had to find a way to support themselves. Fardin says now that it was a combination of their upbringing and the values instilled in them from a young age that enabled them to withstand the hardships. He says that had he not had the mental strength from his upbringing and the attitudes developed in him, he could so easily have dropped out of school and fallen into the temptations that were all around him. In many ways it would have been so much easier to succumb to drugs or alcohol. But he felt a strong motivation and obligation to continue with his education and make something of his life.

'These events made me stronger. A certain stubbornness, which just might be genetic, kept me going through very hard times. I felt always an obligation to do what my father would have wanted me to do, to live my life as he lived his. It is what he did for me and all I can do for him.'

When this book project began, Roshanak was living in Tasmania with her doctor husband. They have two children and now live in Melbourne. Shanna is often asked to speak about her experiences in Iran. On the surface, she has recovered well from that terrible time but she still needs to know that all the doors of the house are locked before she can feel secure.

Once I asked Mrs Moayyad how she feels now, when two of her children are living so far away from her, and she replied proudly, 'We should bring up our children to be citizens of the world. In my religion Bahá'u'lláh said, "The earth is but one country, and mankind its citizens". But it is very hard to be so far away from them.'

Ordinary people, caught up in extraordinary situations, have endured unimaginable horrors and survived, and been able to forgive the perpetrators. They continue to work, and pray, for the unity of all mankind, and the establishment of the Kingdom of God on Earth.

In the beginning my questions were simply:

Is religious freedom sufficient to compensate (given that a compensation is something which can never quite compensate) for the loss of a dear husband and father in such circumstances, and the loss of the life that should have been theirs, in the country of their birth?

How can ordinary people bear the knowledge that something as dreadful as this has been deliberately inflicted on their family? How does it change lives and not destroy them?

Now it seems that the answer can only lie in the incredible strength of the individual's love of God and obedience to what is perceived to be His divine will.

> . . . true Faith is no mere acknowledgement of the Unity of God, but rather the living of a life that will manifest all the perfections and virtues implied in such belief.
>
> ('Abdu'l-Bahá, in *Bahá'í Year Book*, vol. 1, p. 12)

If you have enjoyed this book,

why not read more personal stories?

MANIJEH

Not Only a Change of Name

Manijeh Saatchi with Fereshteh Hooshmand

A story of love, belief and triumph. It is historic because it is the first time that the story of the House of the Báb in Bushehr has been told. It is also Manijeh's story, because she was the custodian of that holy place.

Fereshteh Hooshmand

This book describes a degree of hardship to which very few people are subjected in the course of their lives. Manijeh's beloved husband's untimely death occurs as a consequence of an assault instigated by those opposed to his religious beliefs. Her children are exposed to constant humiliation and discrimination, their education interrupted or terminated. Family assets are confiscated by unscrupulous officials, with no legal justification or redress. Members of her family are reduced to poverty through the operation of schemes designed to deprive them of professional opportunities and income.

However, this is not a book of lamentation; far from it. It is a record of the power of the human spirit to withstand even the most perfidious oppressors and to emerge triumphant from persecution. As such it conveys a message of hope and optimism for all who value truth and who yearn for justice to prevail.

Peter Khan

KNIGHT WITH A BRIEFCASE

The Life of Knight of Bahá'u'lláh Ezzat Zahrai

by Judith Kaye Logsdon-Dubois

Writer Judith Kaye Logsdon-Dubois thought that a businessman's only goal in life was to make as much money as possible and that he could have nothing to say that would interest her – that is, until she met Ezzat Zahrai.

One day she found herself sitting on a terrace of a house in southwest France listening to the former division president of a multinational company speak of spirituality, of visions, of ideals, of mystic experiences, of hardships, prison and persecution, of truth, of destiny, of God. In his youth he had set out alone from Iran for Africa to bring the teachings of the Bahá'í Faith to what is now Zimbabwe for the very first time.

As he told his story, Ms Logsdon-Dubois found Mr Zahrai cared very little about the status of wealth, that he had no taste for luxury. She felt he would have unhesitatingly sacrificed his life for the Faith he believed in. Through his adventures in a new land he had become a modern-day knight, a knight with a briefcase.

Judith Kaye Logsdon-Dubois has captured the essence of Ezzat Zahrai – his humour and good nature, his business ethics, his strong belief in the oneness of humanity and his passion for telling others about the Bahá'í Faith.

AGAINST INCREDIBLE ODDS

Life of a 20th Century Iranian Bahá'í Family

by Baharieh Rouhani Ma'ani

Against Incredible Odds: Life of a 20th Century Iranian Bahá'í Family tells the story of a family from the Iranian town of Nayríz whose life has spanned the whole history of the Bahá'í Faith, from its earliest days to the present. Their story is the story of the Bahá'í Cause itself.

The Rouhani family was a direct witness to the growth of the Bahá'í Faith and also to its persecution, from the time of Bahá'u'lláh, through the ministries of 'Abdu'l-Bahá and Shoghi Effendi and to the establishment and flowering of the Universal House of Justice. At every turn the family faced major misfortunes – fires, floods, the untimely death of their children and spouses, as well as the persecution and difficulties that swept over the Bahá'í community – yet at every turn they served the Faith as its defenders, teachers and pioneers.

It is a story of lifelong struggle against incredible odds, of renouncing worldly pleasures to achieve higher aims, of accepting material deprivations to gain spiritual strength and of forgoing the desire of wanting to be physically close to one's children – the cherished desire of every parent – to enable them to scatter far and wide and work towards the achievement of Bahá'u'lláh's pivotal goal of unifying humankind.

Lightning Source UK Ltd.
Milton Keynes UK
UKHW011056300621
386327UK00008B/313

9 780853 986416